Street by Street

LUTON, DUN

BARTON-LE-CLAY, HARPENDEN, LEIGHTON BUZZARD, REDBOURN, TODDINGTON

Caddington, Eaton Bray, Edlesborough, Harlington, Hexton, Houghton Regis, Kensworth, Linslade, Markyate, Stanbridge, Streatley, Totternhoe, Westoning, Whipsnade

4th edition September 2008
© Automobile Association Developments Limited 2008

Original edition printed May 2001

Enabled by **Ordnance Survey** This product includes map data licensed from Ordnance Survey® with the permission of the Controller of Her Majesty's Stationery Office. © Crown copyright 2008. All rights reserved. Licence number 100021153.

The copyright in all PAF is owned by Royal Mail Group plc.

RoadPilot® DRIVING TECHNOLOGY Information on fixed speed camera locations provided by RoadPilot © 2008 RoadPilot® Driving Technology.

Published by AA Publishing (a trading name of Automobile Association Developments Limited, whose registered office is Fanum House, Basing View, Basingstoke, Hampshire RG21 4EA. Registered number 1878835).

Produced by the Mapping Services Department of The Automobile Association. (A03730)

A CIP Catalogue record for this book is available from the British Library.

Printed by Oriental Press in Dubai

MILTON KEYNES

NORTHAMPTON

SP | TL

Flitwick

Bletchley

Aspley
Heath

Bow
Brickill

Woburn

Eversholt

6 Westoning

Newton
Longville

Potsgrove

10 Harling

Toddington

Hollingdon

16 Heath and Reach **17**

Clipstone

18 **19** **20**

Hockliffe

Wingfield

Tebworth

Chalton

Stewkley

28 Linslade **29** Leighton Buzzard

30 **31** Tilsworth **32** Houg Regis

Burcott

Stanbridge

40 Sewell **41** **42**

Billington

Totternhoe

DUNSTABL

2

Ledburn

50 Eaton Bray **51** **52**

Mentmore

Northall

Church End

Wingrave

Horton

Edlesborough

Whipsnade

Kensw

Hulcott

60

Long
Marston

Pitstone

Dagnall

Jock

Aylesbury

Little
Gaddesden

A41

Buckland

Aldbury

Great
Gaddesden

Tring

Wigginton

Potten
End

Northchurch

SP | TL

National Grid references are shown on the map frame of each page.
Red figures denote the 100 km square and blue figures the 1 km square.
Example, page 5 : Windmill Trading Estate 510 221

The reference can also be written using the National Grid two-letter prefix shown on this page, where 4 and 1 are replaced by TL to give TL1021.

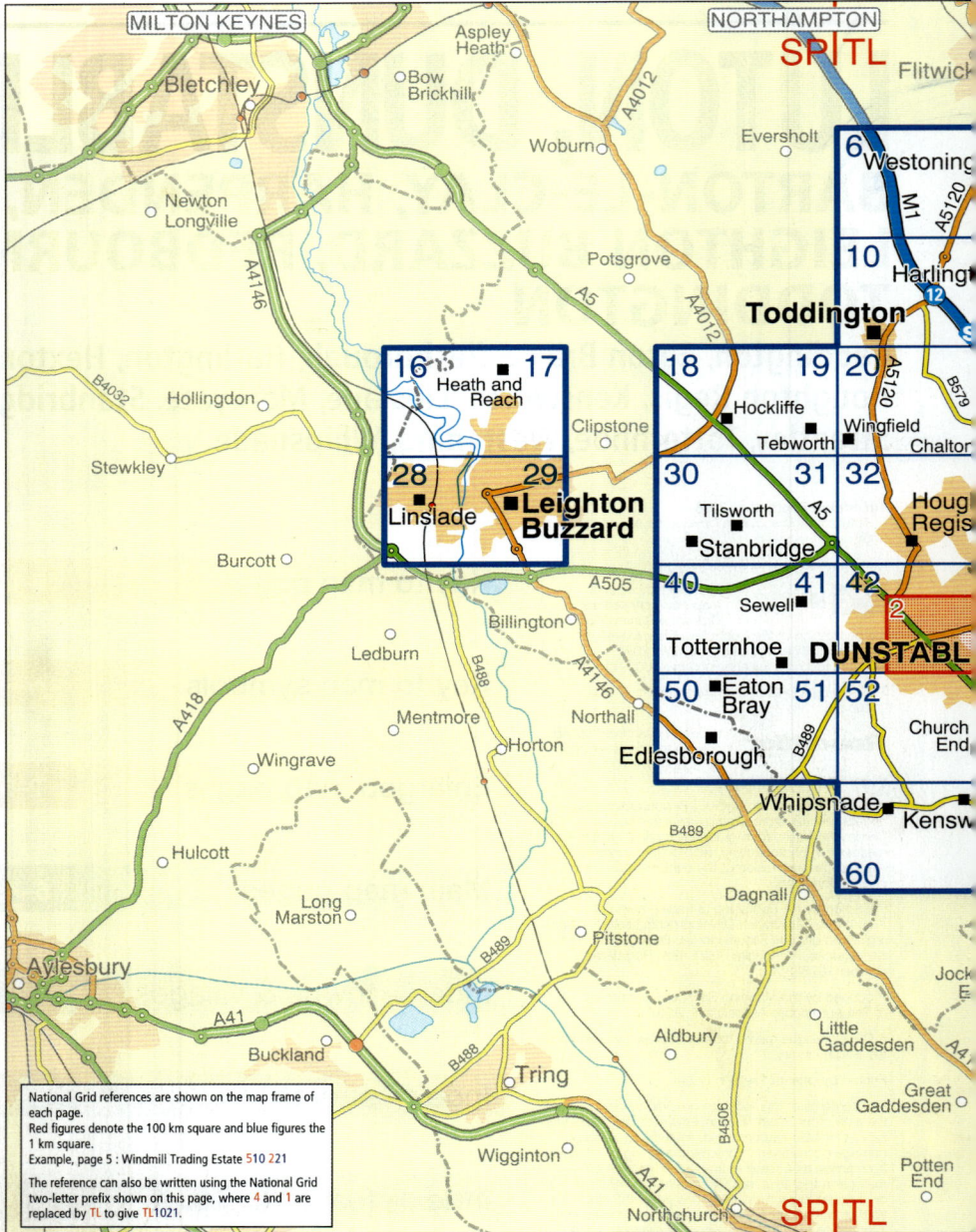

Enlarged scale pages 1:10,000 6.3 inches to 1 mile

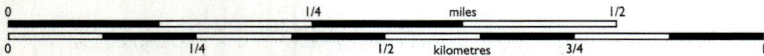

0   1/4   miles   1/2

0   1/4   1/2   kilometres   3/4   1

BEDFORD

Pulloxhill

Shillington

8   9

Apsley End

Holwell

Letchworth Garden City

Baldock

A6
A600
A1(M)

Pirton

Ickleford

Willian

Weston

Barton-le-Clay

Sharpenhoe

13 14   15

Hexton

B655

Hitchin

A505

Graveley

Streatley

Upper Sundon

23 24   25 26   27

A505

Great Offley

Well Head

A602

A1072

8

Stevenage

Lower Sundon

Lilley

Limbury

35 36   37 38   39

B579

Stopsley

Cockernhoe

King's Walden

A6

B656

A1(M)

Shephall

45 46   47 48   49

Breachwood Green

Langley

7

Knebworth

11

A5065

A505

LUTON

Luton

Whitwell

B651

A1(M)

4   5

Caddington

55 56   57 58   59

New Town

Peters Green

Kimpton

Codicote

B656

B197

Welwyn

Slip End

10A

A5

B4540

63 64   65 66   67

East Hyde

B652

M1

A1081

B653

Markyate

68   69 70   71

Batford

Harpenden

B653

Wheathampstead

Welwyn

6

Harmer Green

Friar's Wash

9

A1(M)

A1000

72   73 74   75

Hatching Green

Redbourn

B651

Sandridge

5

Welwyn Garden City

B487

M1

A5183

A1081

Hemel Hempstead

4

WATFORD

HERTFORD

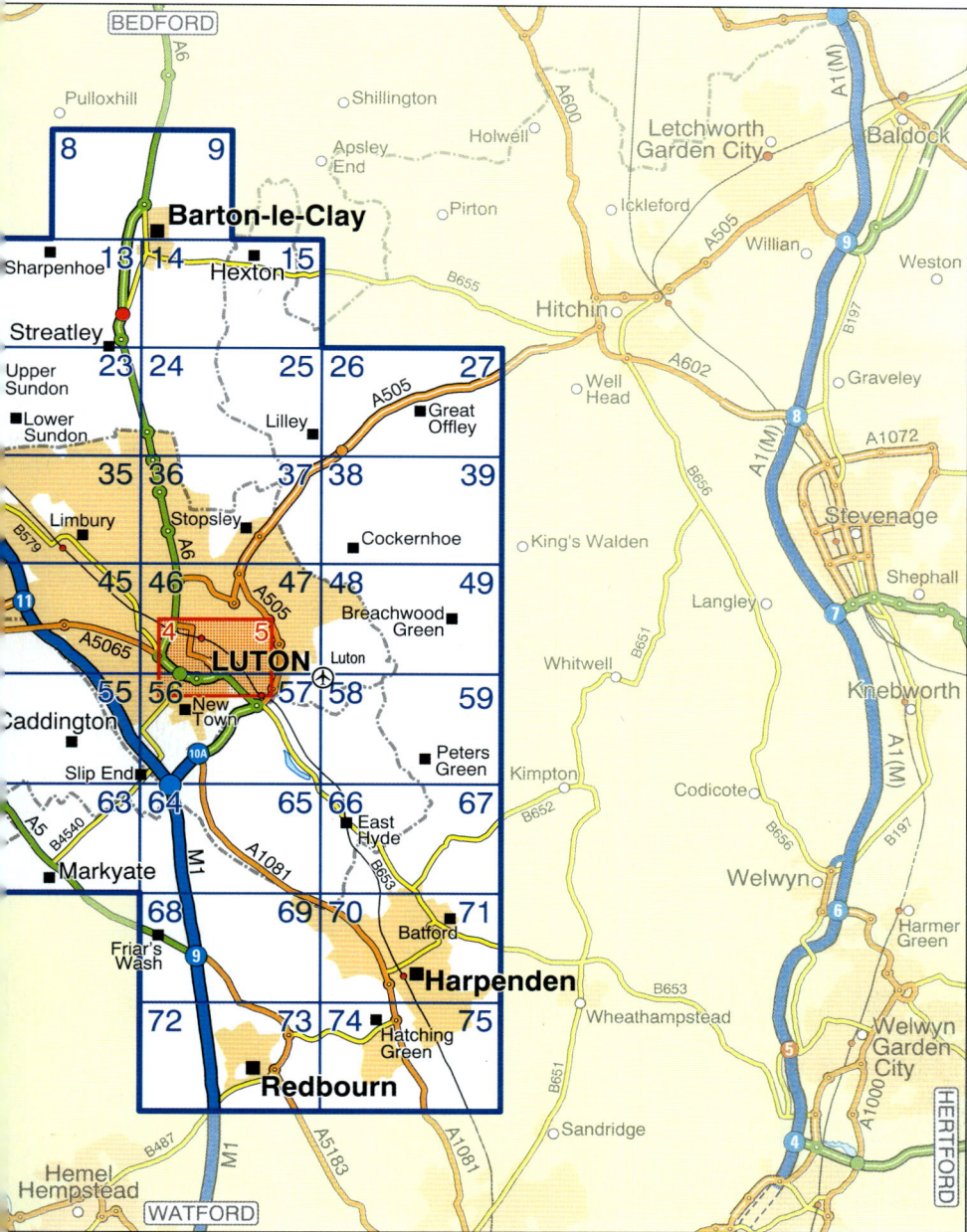

4.2 inches to 1 mile   **Scale of main map pages 1:15,000**

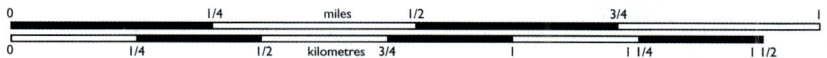

| 0 | 1/4 | miles | 1/2 | 3/4 | 1 |

| 0 | 1/4 | 1/2 | kilometres 3/4 | 1 | 1 1/4 | 1 1/2 |

iv

Junction 9	Motorway & junction		Railway & minor railway station
Services	Motorway service area		Underground station
	Primary road single/dual carriageway		Light railway & station
Services	Primary road service area	++++++++++	Preserved private railway
	A road single/dual carriageway	LC	Level crossing
	B road single/dual carriageway		Tramway
	Other road single/dual carriageway	- - - - - - - - - -	Ferry route
	Minor/private road, access may be restricted	....	Airport runway
← ←	One-way street	- · - · - · -	County, administrative boundary
	Pedestrian area	▼▼▼▼▼▼▼▼▼▼	Mounds
============	Track or footpath	17	Page continuation 1:15,000
	Road under construction	3	Page continuation to enlarged scale 1:10,000
⊢ - - - - ⊣	Road tunnel		River/canal, lake, pier
30	Speed camera site (fixed location) with speed limit in mph		Aqueduct, lock, weir
V	Speed camera site (fixed location) with variable speed limit	465 ▲ Winter Hill	Peak (with height in metres)
40	Section of road with two or more fixed camera sites; speed limit in mph or variable		Beach
50→ ←50	Average speed (SPECS™) camera system with speed limit in mph		Woodland
P	Parking		Park
P+🚌	Park & Ride		Cemetery
🚌	Bus/coach station		Built-up area
	Railway & main railway station		

	Industrial/business building		Abbey, cathedral or priory
	Leisure building		Castle
	Retail building		Historic house or building
	Other building	Wakehurst Place NT	National Trust property
	City wall		Museum or art gallery
A&E	Hospital with 24-hour A&E department		Roman antiquity
PO	Post Office		Ancient site, battlefield or monument
	Public library		Industrial interest
i	Tourist Information Centre		Garden
i	Seasonal Tourist Information Centre		Garden Centre Garden Centre Association Member
	Petrol station, 24 hour Major suppliers only		Garden Centre Wyevale Garden Centre
†	Church/chapel		Arboretum
	Public toilet, with facilities for the less able		Farm or animal centre
PH	Public house AA recommended		Zoological or wildlife collection
	Restaurant AA inspected		Bird collection
Madeira Hotel	Hotel AA inspected		Nature reserve
	Theatre or performing arts centre		Aquarium
	Cinema	V	Visitor or heritage centre
	Golf course		Country park
▲	Camping AA inspected		Cave
	Caravan site AA inspected		Windmill
	Camping & caravan site AA inspected		Distillery, brewery or vineyard
	Theme park	•	Other place of interest

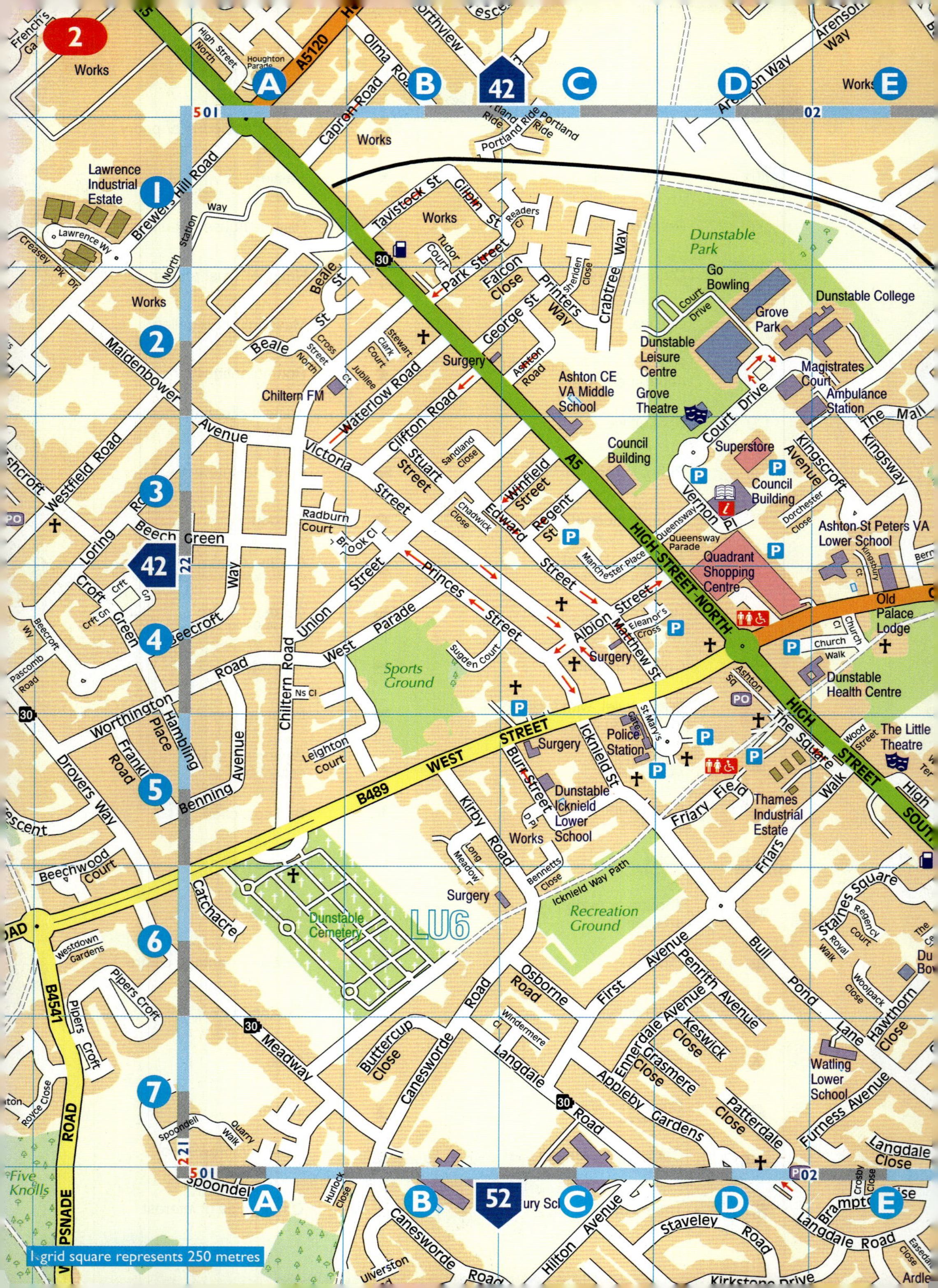

2
Works
Houghton Parade
High Street North
A5120
A5
Olma Road
Northview
42
Arenson Way
Works
Capron Road
Works
Portland Ride
Portland Ride
Lawrence Industrial Estate
Lawrence Wy
Creasey Pk Dr
Brewers Hill Road
North Station Way
Tavistock St
Gilpin St
Readers Cl
Works
Tudor Court
Park Street
Falcon Close
Printers Way
Shenden Close
Crabtree Way
Dunstable Park
Go Bowling
Grove Park
Dunstable College
Court Drive
Works
Maidenbower
Beale St
Beale Street North
Cross Street
Jubilee Ct
Clark Court
Stewart Court
George St
Ashton Road
Surgery
Dunstable Leisure Centre
Magistrates Court
Ambulance Station
Chiltern FM
Waterlow Road
Clifton Road
Ashton CE VA Middle School
Grove Theatre
Court Drive
The Mall
Kingsway
Westfield Road
Avenue
Victoria Street
Stuart Street
Sandland Close
Council Building
Superstore
Kingscroft Avenue
Winfield Street
A5
Vernon Pl
Council Building
Dorchester Close
Loring Road
Beech Green
Radburn Court
Brook Cl
Chadwick Close
Edward Street
Regent St
Queensway Parade
Ashton St Peters VA Lower School
Croft Green
Way
Union Street
Princes Street
Manchester Place
HIGH STREET NORTH
Quadrant Shopping Centre
Kingsbury
Old Palace Lodge
Beecroft Way
Beecroft
West Parade
Albion Street
Eleanor's Cross
Church St
Church Walk
Pascomb Road
Chiltern Road
Road
West
Sports Ground
Sugden Court
Matthew St
Surgery
Ashton Sq
Dunstable Health Centre
Worthington Road
Hambling Place
Franklin Road
Ns Cl
Icknield St
Police Station
St Mary's Gate
The Square
Wood Street
The Little Theatre
Drovers Way
Benning Avenue
Leighton Court
B489 WEST STREET
Burr Street
Surgery
Dunstable Icknield Lower School
Friary Field
Thames Industrial Estate
Walk
HIGH STREET SOUTH
Crescent
Kirby Road
Long Meadow
Works
Friars
Beechwood Court
Catchacre
Bennetts Close
Icknield Way Path
Staines Square
Regency Court
Royal Walk
Westdown Gardens
Dunstable Cemetery
LU6
Surgery
Recreation Ground
Bull Pond Lane
Woolpack Close
Hawthorn Close
B4541
Pipers Croft
Pipers Croft
Meadway
Buttercup Close
Canesworde Road
Osborne Road
First Avenue
Penrith Avenue
Ennerdale Avenue
Keswick Close
Windermere Cl
Langdale Road
Grasmere Close
Appleby Gardens
Watling Lower School
Furness Avenue
Patterdale Close
Royce Close
ROAD
Spoondell
Quarry Walk
Langdale Close
Crosby Close
Five Knolls
WHIPSNADE
Spoondell
Hurlock Close
52
Canesworde Road
Hilton Avenue
Staveley Road
Langdale Road
Brampton Rise
Easedale Close
Ulverston
Kirkstone Drive
Ardle
1 grid square represents 250 metres

Verey
Woodside Industrial Estate
Road
Eyncourt
Humber
Helmwo
Goldstone Crescent
Avenue
43
Hadrian
Duncombe Drive
Lockington
Millers
Crescent
Evelyn
Hob Road

F G H J K

Chiltern Park
Chiltern Park Industrial Estate
Hadrian Lower School
Cattereys
Pynders Lane
Katherine
Lay
Drive
Linden
Walgrave Road
Thornbury
Gorham

White Lion Retail Park
Boscombe Road
Ridgeway Avenue
Chalk Acres
Hillcrest Special School
Florence Ct
Monks Close
Brandreth Avenue
Woodford Rd
Wingate Road
Buckwood Avenue
St Chri
2
Linden Close

Lukeminster ading tate
Superstore
LU5
Bramley Court
Chiltern Park Industrial Estate
Western Way
The Crest
Ridgeway Drive
PO
Fairfield Road
Fairfield Close
A505
30
The Retreat

Luton Road
LUTON ROAD
30
Parrot Close
Kingsbury Avenue
3
Kingsbury Gardens
43
Icknield Way Path

30 STREET
Works
St Peter's
Station Rd
Road
Alfred Street
Englands Lane
Great Northern Road
Eastern Avenue
Luton Road
Liscombe Road
Eastern Avenue Industrial Estate
Jeans
Ludon Works
Ludon Close
4

Long Hedge
Woodside Clinic
Oak
Ash
Limewalk
Icknield Way Path
DUNSTABLE
5

Street
Richard St
Allen Close
Sports Ground

Kers' Walk
King Street
Great Northern Road
Grove Road
Downs Road
Barton Avenue
6

Albert Court
Works
Great Park Road
Blows Road
Lane
Chichester Close
Apollo Close
Downside Lower School
PO
Borough Road
Howard Place
Moon
Norcott Close
Jardine Way
Graham Road
7

A5
Willoughby Cl
Half
Sundown Avenue
Hillside
Mayfield Road
Avenue
Brive Road
Bowmans Way
Bowmans Close
LONDON ROAD
Index Drive
Tolbert Close
Grovebury Cl
Graphic Cl
Oakwood
Southwood Road
221

F G H J K
Turnpike Close
53
May Road
Mountview
New Woodfield Green
Downside
Works
Highwayman Hotel

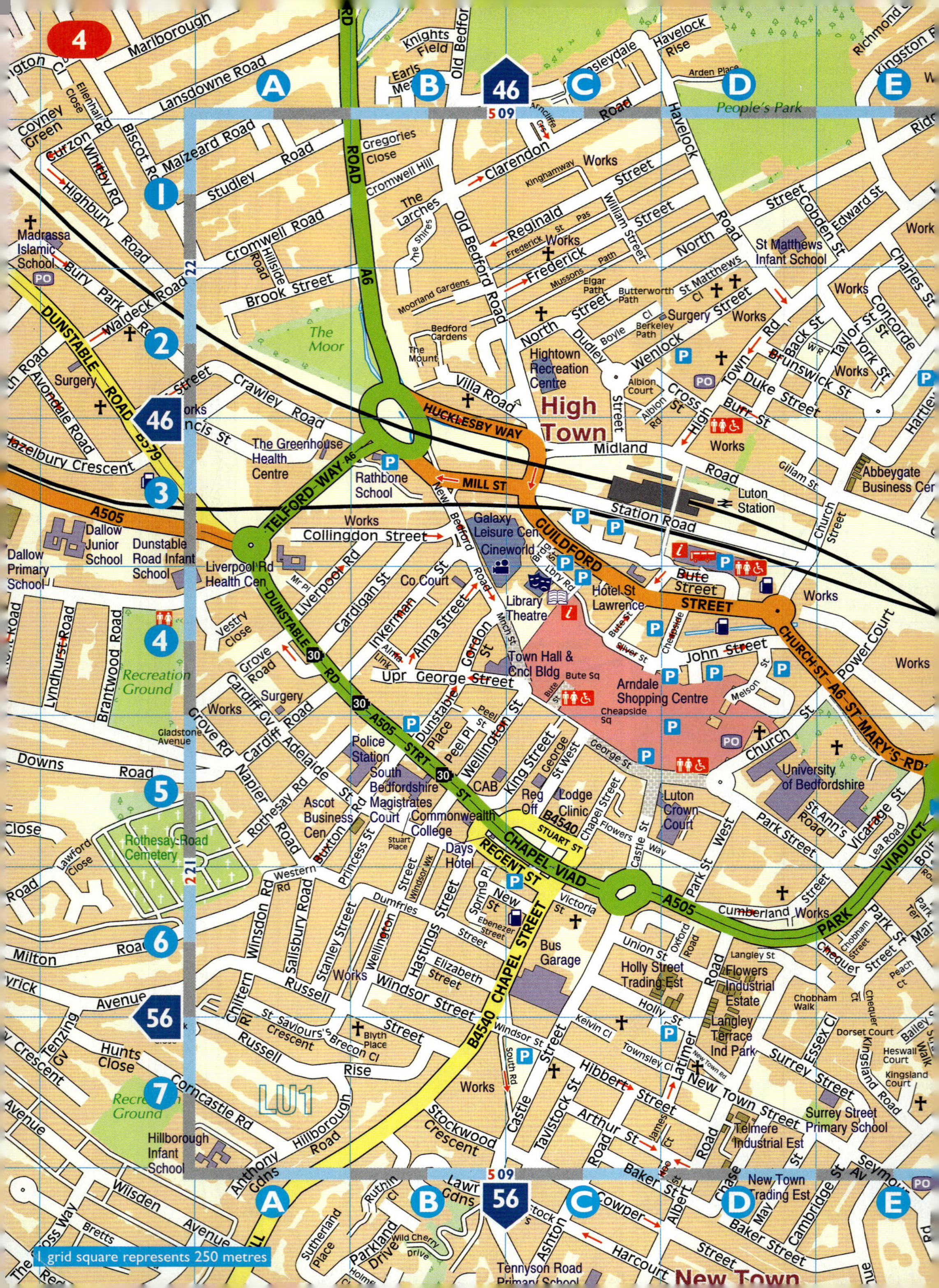

Map grid references

A B 46 C D E

I 2 46 3 4 5 56 6 7

Marlborough
Lansdowne Road
Knights Field
Earls Mead
Old Bedford Road
Cleydale
Havelock Rise
Arden Place
People's Park
Richmond
Kingston Rd

Coyney Green
Elenhall
Curzon Rd
Whitby Rd
Highbury
Malzeard Road
Gregories Close
Cromwell Hill
The Larches
The Shires
Clarendon
Kinghamway
Works
Street
Street
Street
Cobden St
Edward St
Work

Madrassa Islamic School
Bury Park
Waldeck Road
Cromwell Road
Hillside Road
Brook Street
Reginald St
Frederick Works
Frederick
Mussons Path
Elgar Path
Butterworth
St Matthews Cl
North
Street
Street
Dudley
Boyle
Berkeley Path
St Matthews
Surgery Street
Works
St Matthews Infant School
Charles St
Concorde
Taylor York St

DUNSTABLE ROAD
Surgery
46
B579
Francis St
The Moor
Moorland Gardens
Bedford Gardens
The Mount
Villa Road
North Street
Wenlock
High Town
Albion Court
Town
Duke Street
Brunswick St
Hartley

Hazelbury Crescent
A505
Crawley Road
HUCKLESBY WAY
Midland
High
Street
Cross St
Albion Rd
Burr St
Abbeygate Business Cen
Gilliam St

Dallow Junior School
Dunstable Road Infant School
TELFORD WAY A6
The Greenhouse Health Centre
Rathbone School
MILL ST
New
Bedford
Station Road
Luton Station
Church Street
Works

Dallow Primary School
Liverpool Rd Health Cen
Collingdon Street
Works
Liverpool Rd
Galaxy Leisure Cen
Cineworld
GUILDFORD
Bute Street
STREET
CHURCH ST A6 ST MARY'S RD
Power Court

Vestry Close
DUNSTABLE RD
Cardigan St
Co Court
Inkerman
Alma Street
Gordon
Minch St
Library & Theatre
Hotel St Lawrence
Cheapside
John Street
Melson St
Works

Recreation Ground
Lyndhurst Road
Brantwood Road
Grove Road
Cardiff Gv
Surgery
30
A505 DUNSTABLE ST RD
Upr George Street
Town Hall & Cncl Bldg
Arndale Shopping Centre
Cheapside Sq
Bute Sq
Church
University of Bedfordshire

Gladstone Avenue
Cardiff Rd
Adelaide St
Works
Peel St
Wellington St
King Street
George St
George St
John St West
Park St West
Park Street
Vicarage Rd
St Ann's Rd
Lea Road
VIADUCT

Downs Road
Napier Rd
Police Station
South Bedfordshire Magistrates Court
30
CAB
Reg Off
Lodge Clinic
Luton Crown Court
Church
PO

Rothesay Road Cemetery
Ascot Business Cen
Commonwealth College
Stuart Place
Buxton
B540
Stuart St
Castle
Chapel St
Flowers Way
PARK
Park Rd
Chequer Street

Lawford Close
Western Rd
Days Hotel
Princess St
CHAPEL VIAD
REGENT ST
A505
Cumberland Works
Chobham Walk

Milton Avenue
Kenzing Gv
Chiltern Rd
Stanley Road
Salisbury Road
St Saviour's Crescent
Wellington Street
Spring Pl
Ebenezer street
New Bute St
Victoria
CHAPEL STREET
Bus Garage
Union St
Oxford St
Langley St
Holly Street Trading Est
Langley Terrace Ind Park
Dorset Court
Heswall Court
Kingsland Court

Hunts Close
Russell Street
Brecon Cl
Blyth Place
Windsor Road
South Rd
Holly
Flowers Industrial Estate
Surrey Street
Essex St
Kingsland Road
Balley's

Hillborough Infant School
Recreation Ground
LU1
Corncastle Rd
Hillborough Road
Stockwood Crescent
Windsor Street
Works
Kelvin Cl
Townsley Cl
Hibbert Street
Arthur Street
Tavistock St
New Town Street
New Town
Telmere Industrial Est
Surrey Street Primary School

Wisden Road
Anthony Gdns
Wilsden Avenue
Ruffin Rd
Lawr Gdns
Parkland Drive
Wild Cherry drive
56
Cowper St
Ashton Rd
Baker Street
Albert Rd
New Town Trading Est
Cambridge St
Seymour Av
PO

Tennyson Road Primary School
Harcourt Street
New Town

1 grid square represents 250 metres

F G H 47 J K

Winch Road
St
Kenneth Rd
Cherry Tree
Bloomfield
Stanford Av
set
Avenue
ell Road
A50
Carteret

The Business Centre
The 10

Abbey
Abbots
Exton
Road
Road
Avenue
Highover Close

Vauxhall Way
Falconers Rd
2 21
Brendon
Porlock Drive
Hollybush Road
High Ridge

Town
Oxen Industrial Estate

Hart Hill

Hart Lane
Hart Wk
Wood Drive
Taunton Avenue
Eaton
Valley
Plymouth Close

I

Works
LU2
Tower Wy
Cowridge Crescent
Crawley Green Road
Devon
Buchanan
Road
Drive

A50

2

Polzeath Close
Avenue

47

Hart Hill Primary School

Pomfret Avenue
Tower Road
Derwent Road
Brooms Road
Whitecroft Road
Leygreen Close
Wenlock Junior School
Crawley Green Infant School
Gayland Av
Devon Road

Harrowden Road
Eaton
3
Works

Haddon Road
Hart Hill
Hart Hill
Lane
Farnley Gv
Hl La
Crawley Green Road
Blaydon Rd
Durham
Silecroft Road
Beaconsfield
Road
Works
4
Prospect Wy

Works
Road
30
30
Rutland Crescent
Norfolk Road
Ketton Cl
Devon Road

Vicks Rd

Luton Church Cemetery

5

Works

Thistle Rd
Windmill Trading Estate

Windmill Rd
A505

creation und

6
Works

ON

P

P
Works
Kimpton
Road
57

Park Town

A505
Road
Luton Retail Park
Works
Road
Barratt
Park
7

Osborne
Premier Inn
Gipsy Lane
P
Luton Airport Parkway Station
Road
Vauxhall
AIR

Park Street
River Lea or Lee
Parkway Rd
P
Vauxhall

F G H 57 J K
10
11

6

500 · 01

A · **B** · **C** · **D**

Town
Farm

1

Tingrith Road

33

Hill's Plantation

Priestley Plantation

Redcaps

2

32

Church Road

St Nicholas Close

High Street

Tingrith

3

Woo

4

Harlington
Wood End

Daintry
Wood

5

Long Lane
Farm

231

M1

500 · 01

A · **B** · **10** · **C** · **D**

Lodge
Farm

Long Lane

1 grid square represents 500 metres

E F G H

03 04

I

DUNSTA...

FLITWICK ROAD A5120

...nix School

2

Manor House

Church Rd

John Bunyan Trail

The Gv

Church Road

Manor Gardens

Highfields

Flitwick Road

Church Cl

HIGH ST

Bell Close

Greenfield Road

Clayhill Farm

Cemetery

HW5 La

Tyburn Lane

Rchm

Ty Br Cl

Manor Park Dr

Sanderson Road

Westoning Lower School

Westoning

Oak

The Pound

PO

Home Farm Way

PARK ROAD

Balcony

Newlands

Sampshill Road

Campion Road

Bunyan Road

3

Manor Close

60

Kerr

Spensley Rd

Robin...

4

John Bunyan Trail

Westoning Road

33

32

5

Goswell End Road

Harlington Upper School

A.231

E F **II** G H

03 04

Brwn's

S wy

Glebe Gdns

Westoning Road

Lower School

Wingate Road

Dbny Cl

Monmouth

Lincoln Way

Foster Rd

Bunya...

Churchill

Brian Road

Bunya Walk

PO

Redhills Farm

nd

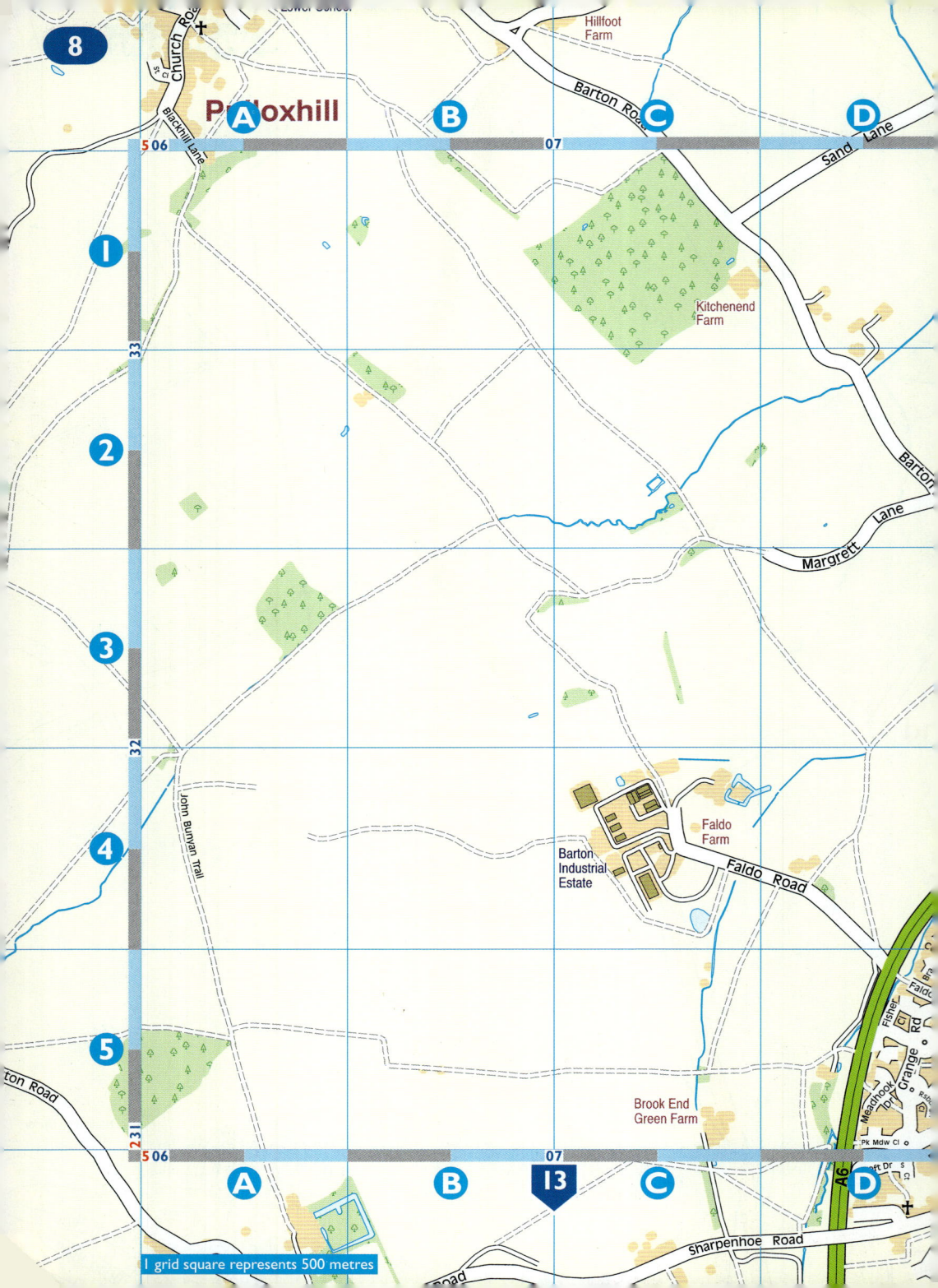

Church Road

St

Cl

+

Blackhill Lane

P Hoxhill

Lower Street

Hillfoot
Farm

Barton Road

Sand Lane

Barton

A

B

C

D

5 06

07

33

I

Kitchenend
Farm

2

Margrett

Lane

Barton

3

32

John Bunyan Trail

4

Faldo
Farm

Barton
Industrial
Estate

Faldo Road

5

ton Road

2 31

Brook End
Green Farm

Fisher

Grange

Faldo

Cl

Rd

Meadhook Top

Pk Mdw Cl

ert Dr

S

A6

5 06

07

A

B

I3

C

D

Sharpenhoe Road

Road

E F G H

New Inn Farm

Fielden House

A6

I

33

Manor Farm

Manor Farm Business Park

2

Westhey Manor

Higham Road

3

32

4

Higham Road

Hanover Pl

Stuart Road

Windsor Road

Bedford Road

Cromwell Road

Norman Road

Hastings Road

Harold Rd

Dane Road

Roman Rd

York Close

Kg William Close

Saxon Cts

L Cl

B655

BEDFORD ROAD

Manor Road

The Coach House

White Hl Rd

Ramsey Rd

Grays Close

Lime

Crutte

BARTON-LE-CLAY

John Bunyan Trail

5

231

John Bunyan Tr

E F 14 G H

PO

Bradshaws Cl

Arnold Close

Apple Glebe

Hexton Rd

Dunstall Road

Manor Road

Blakelands

Osborn Road

Ramsey Manor Lower School

Arnold Middle School

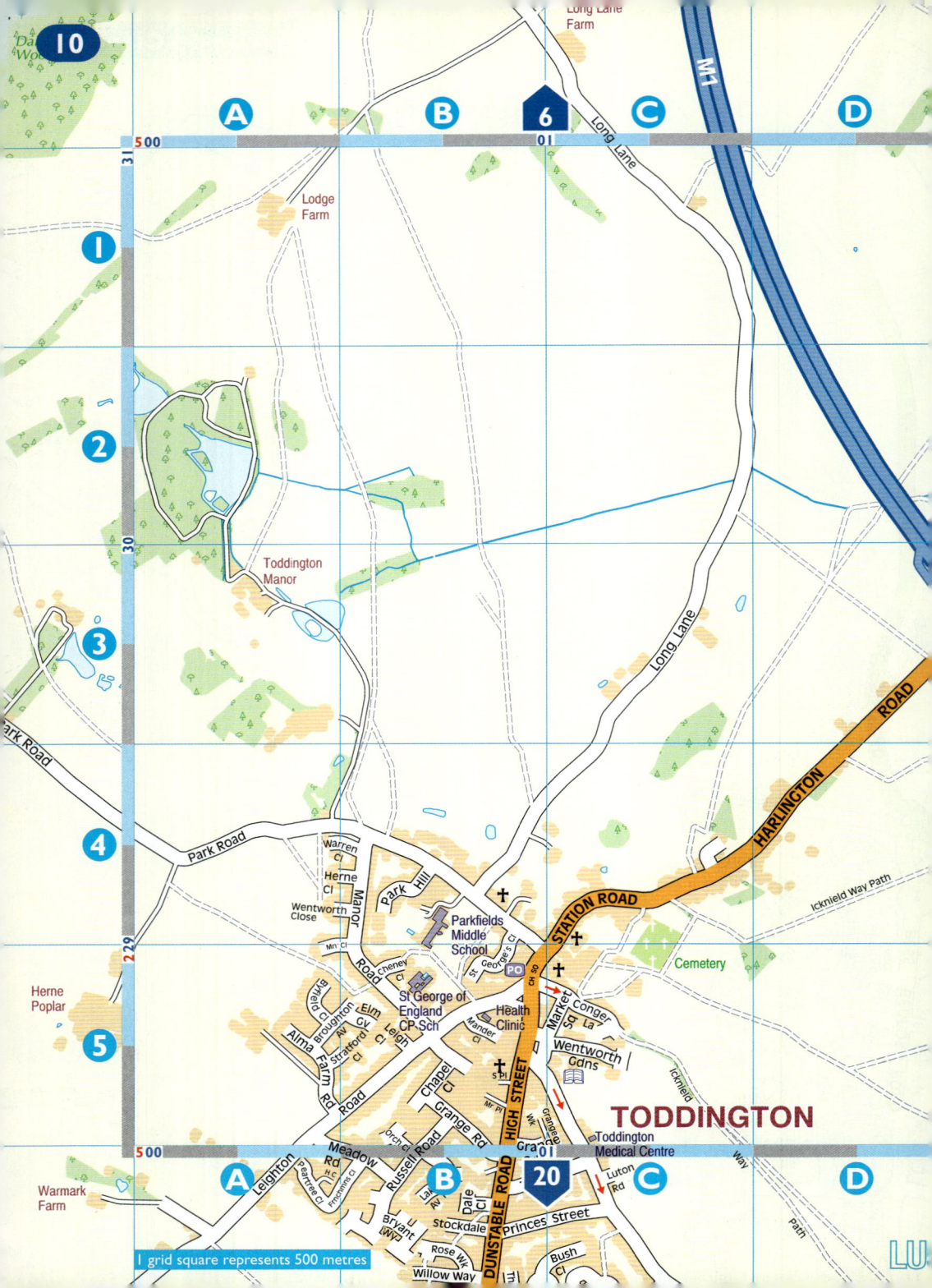

Da
Wo

A B 6 C D
01

M1

5 00
31

Long Lane
Farm

Long Lane

Lodge
Farm

I

2

30

Toddington
Manor

3

Long Lane

Park Road

HARLINGTON ROAD

4

Park Road

Warren
Cl

Herne
Cl

Manor Road

Park Hill

Wentworth
Close

Parkfields
Middle
School

Mn Cl

Cheney
Cl

STATION ROAD

Icknield Way Path

Cemetery

2 29

Herne
Poplar

Byfield

Broughton Av

Elm
Gv

Stratford Cl

Leigh

St George of
England
CP.Sch

St George's Cl

PO
CH SQ

Health
Clinic

Mander
Cl

Market
Conger
La

Icknield

5

Alma Farm Rd

Chapel
Cl

Rose

Road

Grange Rd

Grange

S Pl

Mr Pl

WK

Wentworth
Gdns

Orange Cl

High Street

TODDINGTON

Toddington
Medical Centre

5 00

A Leighton B C D
20

Meadow
Rd

Russell Road

H Cl

Peartree Cl

Finchmere Cl

Dale
La

Stockdale

DUNSTABLE ROAD

Princes Street

Luton
Rd

Way

Path

Warmark
Farm

Orch Cl

Bryant
Wy

Rose Wy

Bush

Willow Way

LU

E   F   **7**   03   G   Goswell End Road   **H**   04   Harlington Upper School

Redhills Farm

Westoning Road

Brwn's
Robinson Crts
s Wy
Ciebe Gdns
Lower School
Wingate Road
Dbny Cl
Foster Rd
Bunyans
Churchills
Churchill Road
Tabor Cl
Walk
A C
Cemetery
PO
I
Brian Road
Barton Road

Toddington   Road

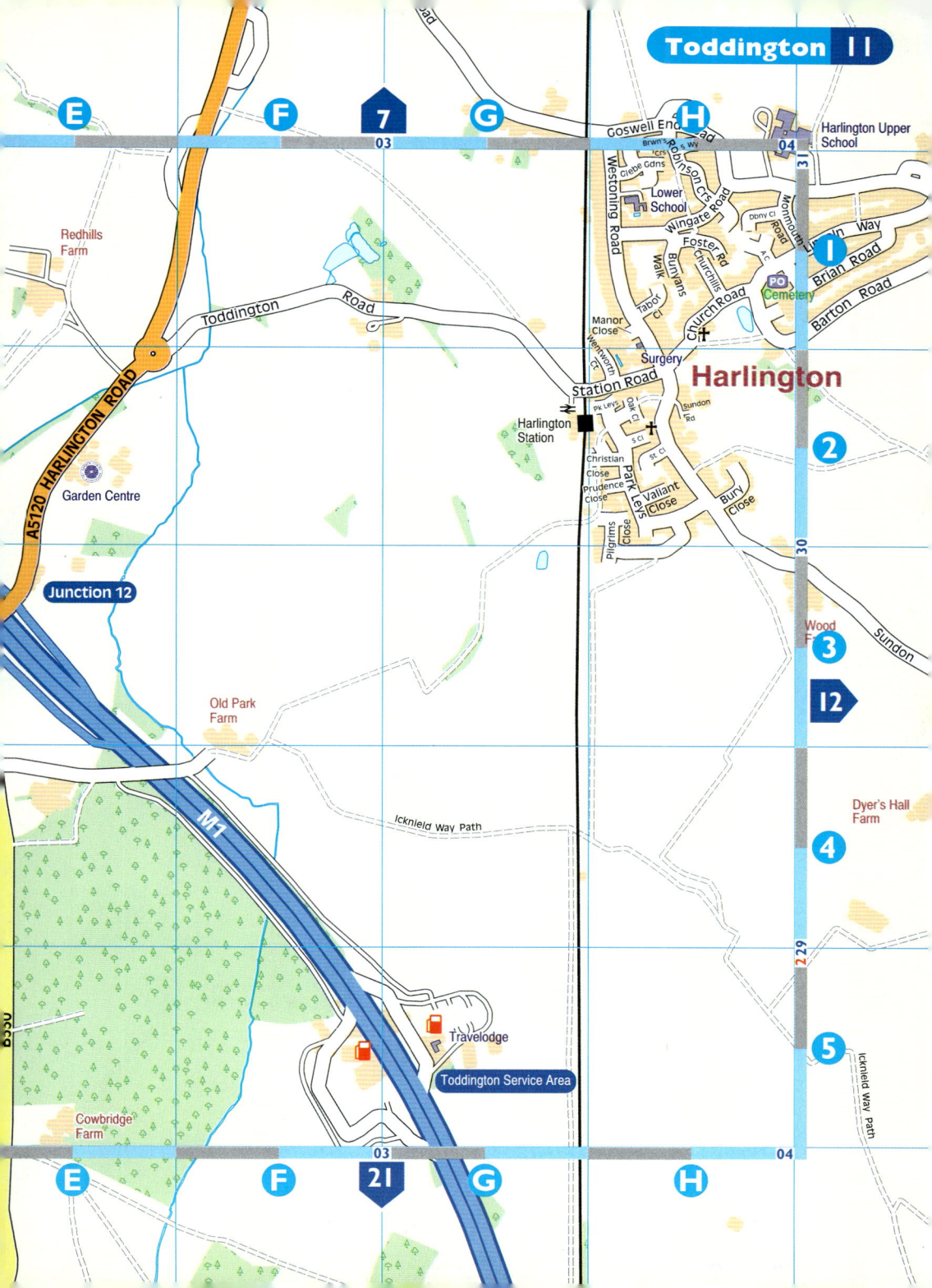

Manor Close
Wentworth
Surgery
Church Road
Harlington
Sundon Rd

Station Road
Pk Leys
Park Leys
St Cl
S Cl
St Cl
Harlington Station
2

Garden Centre

Christian Close
Prudence Close
Park Leys
Valiant Close
Bury Close

A5120 HARLINGTON ROAD

Pilgrims Close

30

Junction 12

Wood F'
3
Sundon

Old Park Farm

12

Icknield Way Path

Dyer's Hall Farm

M1

4

2 29

5
Icknield Way Path

Travelodge

Toddington Service Area

Cowbridge Farm

E   F   03   **21**   G   04   **H**

12

A B C D

Grange Farm

Harlington Road

Harlington Upper School

Harlington Road

504

05

nd Road

Robinson Crs

Wy

hool

Wingate Road

Foster Rd

Bunyans

Monmouth Road

Churchills Road

Church Road

Dbny Cl

Lincoln Way

Brian Road

Barton Road

1

PO

Cemetery

East End Farms

Harlington

Sundon Rd

2

Bury Close

ant ose

31

30

3

Wood Farm

Sundon Road

11

Dyer's Hall Farm

4

229

Sundon Road

Sundon Hills Country Park

5

Icknield Way Path

Icknield Way Path

Icknield Way Path

Harlington Road

SH

504

05

A B **22** C D

Holtwood Farm

1 grid square represents 500 metres

E F 9 G H
07 08

I

Sharpenhoe 13

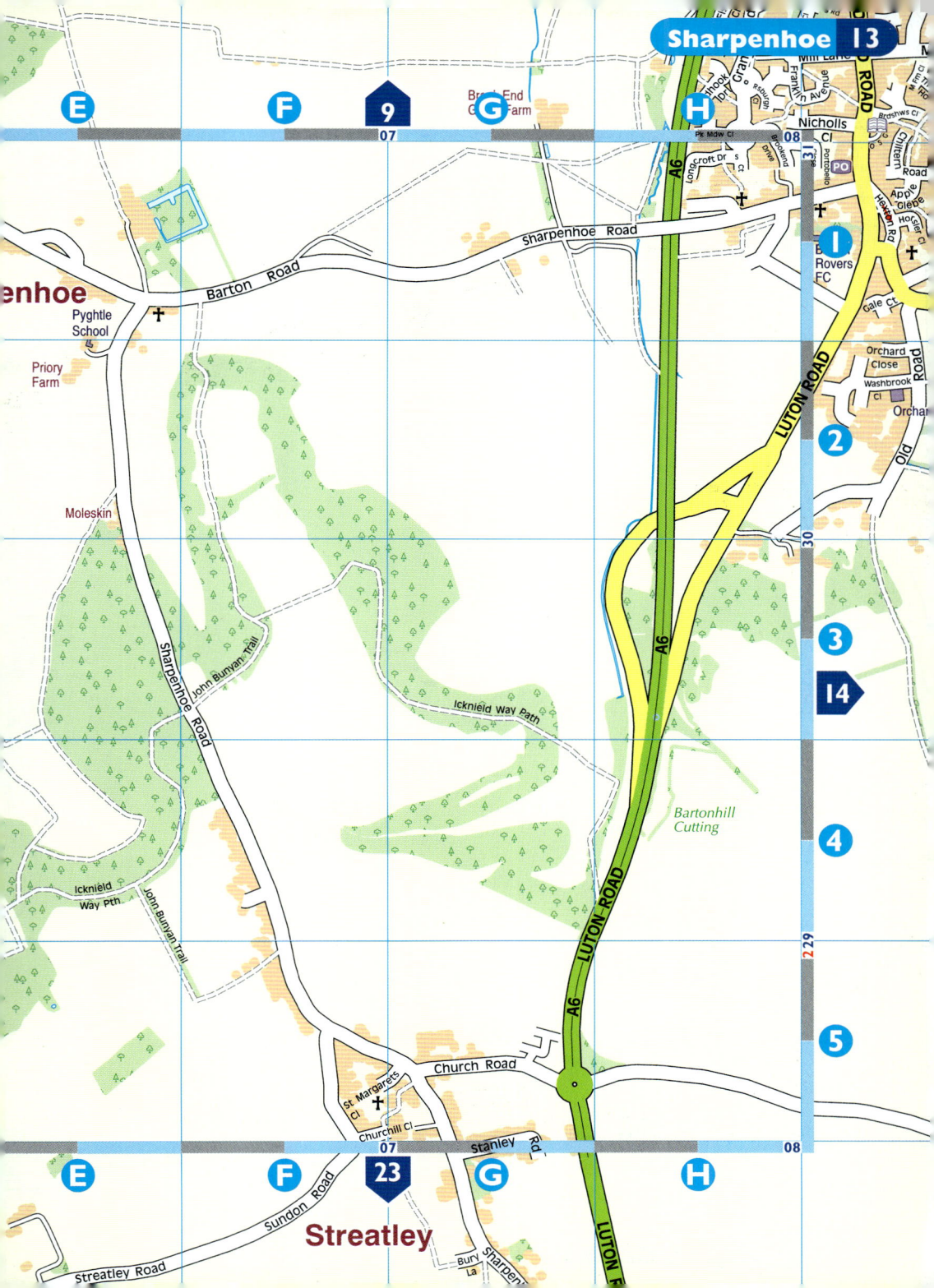

Brache End Farm

Nicholls

Pk Mdw Cl

Mill Lane

Granby

Franklin Ave

Rathbury

Brtshws Cl

Chiltern Road

PO

Portobello

Long Croft Dr

Brookend

Droved

Hexton Rd

Hoster Rd

Apple Glebe

Sharpenhoe Road

Barton Road

enhoe

Pyghtle School

Priory Farm

Moleskin

Sharpenhoe Road

John Bunyan Trail

Icknield Way Path

Icknield Way Pth

John Bunyan Trail

A6

LUTON ROAD

A6

Gale Ct

Orchard Close

Washbrook Cl

Orchar

2

30

3

14

Bartonhill Cutting

4

22 29

5

LUTON ROAD

A6

Church Road

St Margarets Cl

Churchill Cl

Stanley Rd

LUTON

E F 23 G H
07 08

Streatley

Sundon Road

Streatley Road

Bury La

Sharpen

B Rovers FC

BARTON-LE-CLAY

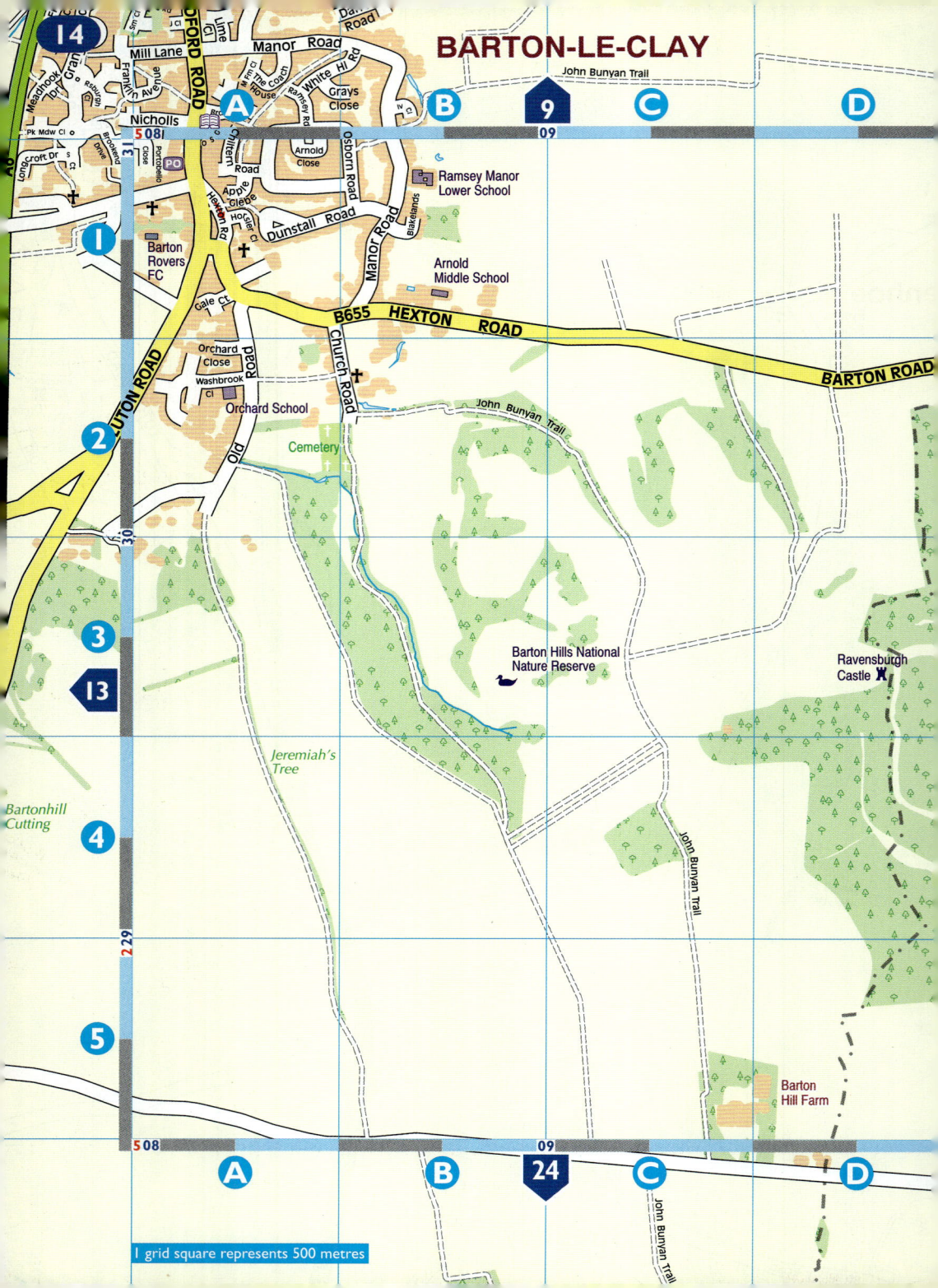

14

Mill Lane
Manor Road
Lime
BEDFORD ROAD
Grans
Meadhook
Franklin Avenue
Rsburgn
Pk Mdw Cl
Browed
Brookend
Long Croft Dr

A Nicholls
5 081
31
Chiltern Close
PO
Portobello
Apple Glebe
Dunstall Road
Hexton Rd
Hosler Rd
Road
White Hl Rd
Ramsey Rd
Arnold Close
Grays Close
Osborn Road

B
John Bunyan Trail
9
09
C
D

Barton Rovers FC
Gale Ct
Road
LUTON ROAD
2
Orchard Close
Washbrook Cl
Orchard School
Old Road
Church Road
B655 HEXTON ROAD
Ramsey Manor Lower School
Blakelands
Arnold Middle School
BARTON ROAD

30
Cemetery
John Bunyan Trail

3

13
Jeremiah's Tree

Barton Hills National Nature Reserve

Ravensburgh Castle

Bartonhill Cutting
4

John Bunyan Trail

2 29

5

Barton Hill Farm

5 08
A
B
24
09
C
John Bunyan Trail
D

I grid square represents 500 metres

E F Mill Lane G H

Manor Farm

Hexton

PH
PO

Hexton Manor

Hexton Primary School

Bury Farm

Pegsdon

Pegsdon Way

BARTON   ROAD   HITCHIN ROAD

The Meg

Gravel Hill

Fairy Hole

Icknield Way Path

Bedfor... He...

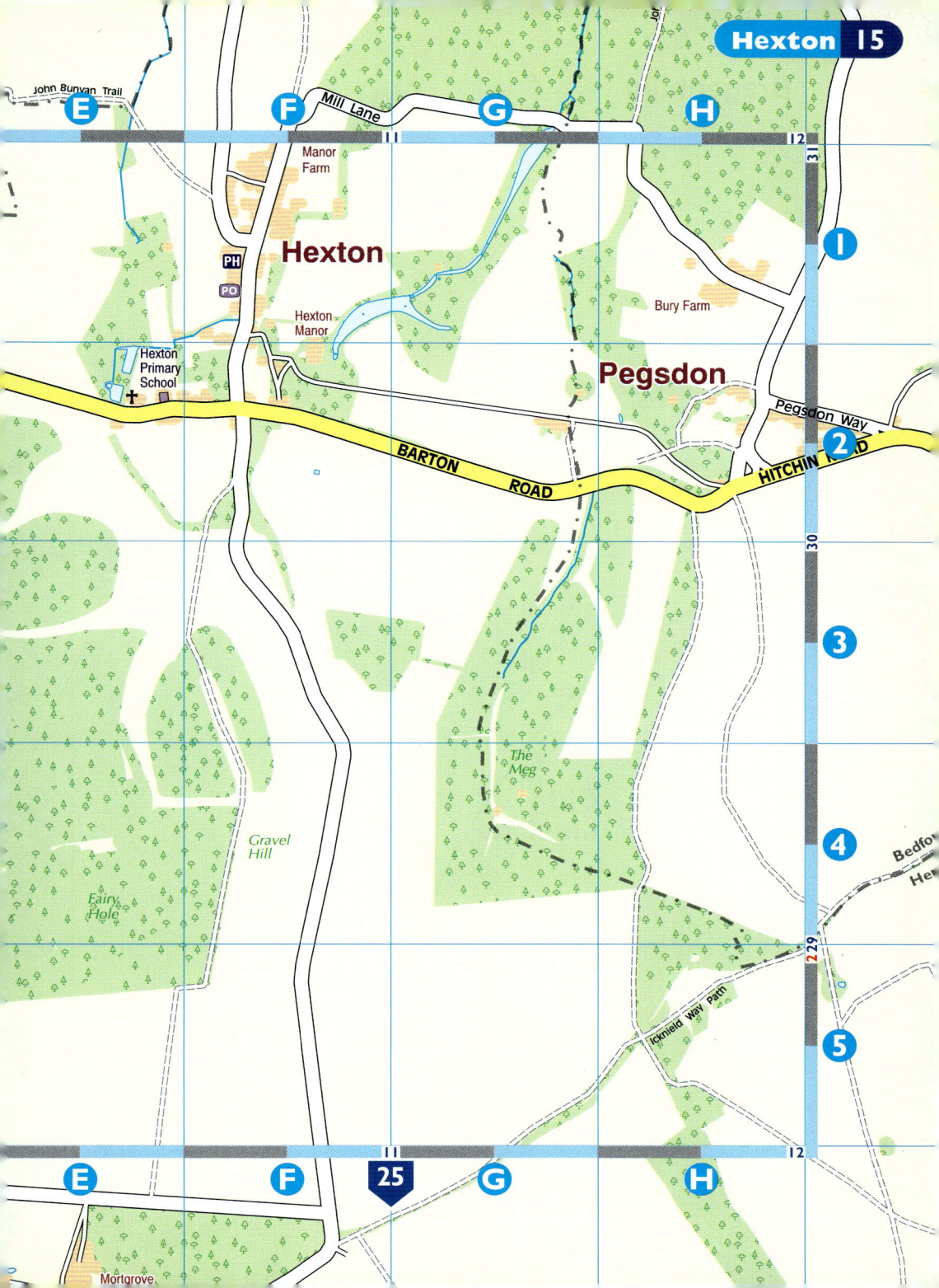

John Bunyan Trail

E F 25 G H

Mortgrove

16

Bragenham

A   B   C   D

4 90

I

bleford

28

2

River Ouzel

Grand Union Canal

Bragenham Lane

Linslade

Rushmere

Grand Union Canal Walk

Greensand Rdg Wk

The Heath

Leighton Buzza
Golf Club

Heath Court

Dukes Ride

3

Broad Oak

Cross Bucks Way

Grand Union Canal

Redw

Oxendon Ct

Robins Ct

27

Taylor's

Woodland Av

4

Leighton Road

**Old
Linslade**

Old Linslade Road

Cem

†

Greensand Ridge Walk

5

Buckinghamshire County

Bedfordshire County

Stoke Road

Globe Lane

PH Grand Union Canal Walk

Works

2 26

4 90

Valley
Farm

A   B   28   C   D

4 90   91

Chestnut
Rise

Cleveland Drive

Malvern

Milebush

Bideford

Soulbur

Chestnut Hill

Alwins Field

Knaves Hill

Hill

Row

Furrows

Uppr Cmb

Lincombe Slade

Bossington Lane

Martins Drive

Rothschild Road

Works

Princes

I grid square represents 500 metres

E · F · G · H · I

93 · 94

Heath and Reach

Works
Werena Farm
Green Lane

St Leonards Heath & Reach VA Sch
Thrift Road
Thomas St
Woburn Road
Grange Gdns
Reach Lane
Works
sheepcote Crs
Bird's Hill
Sylvester St
PO
The Dell
Emu
Pinkle Hill Rd
Gig Lane
Rushings
The Stile
Lane's End
Heath Green
Abbey Wk
Evans Yd
Eastern Way

Golf Course

Leighton Road

2

Craddocks Dr
Oak Bank Special School
Oak Bank Drive
Shenley Close
Shenley Gardens
St Leonard's
Chiltern
Carlton Gv
Shenley Hill Road
Stonehenge Works Station
Mile Tree Road
3
Sandy Lane
30
Heathwood Lower Sch
Heath Park Road
Heathwood Close
Heath Rd
Copper Beech Way
Heath Park
Heath Park Dr
Pine Close
The Walnuts
Cotefield Drive
Dovery Down Lower School
Poplar Close
Broomhills Farm
LC
27

Hillside Road
Heath Road
Adams Bottom
Path
Chamberlains Gdns
Leighton Buzzard Railway
4

Greenhill
Shepherds Md
Woburn Pl
Broomhills Road
Badgers Brook
Plantation Road
Carnation Close
Northcourt
Winston Cl
Churchill Road
Tindall Av
Montgomery Cl
Oakley
Mntbttn Gdns
Nelson Road
Vandyke Rd
LC
30
Vandyke Road
Vandyke Upper School & Comm Coll
Gilbert Inglefield Middle School
5
2 26

93 · 94
Clipstone

E · F · G · H
Riverside
Clarence Road
PO
Pennivale Cl
Heath Road
Mtr
29
Hornbeam
Meadway
Green
Willow Bank Wk
Columba Dr
Phoenix Cl
Hydrus Dr
Appenine Way
Beaudesert Lower School
Roosevelt Av
St Georges Lower School
Ash Gv
Almond Rd
Dove Tree Rd
Omega Rd
Ariel
Saturn Cl
Gemini Close
Centauri Cl
Lyra Gdns
Jupiter
Mercury Way
Orion Way
ng Street
Digby Rd
Talbot Ct
East St
Pear

LEIGHTON BUZZARD

18

Battlesden

A 496 B 97 C D

1

28

2

Hill Farm

3

Hockliffe Grange

27

Church Lane

Church End

Cemetery

Hockliffe Lower School

A5

Grange Farm

Goose Green

Augustus Rd

WOBURN ROAD

Manor Avenue

White Horse Ct

Nine Lambs

Hockliffe

HOCKLIFFE ROAD

A4012

4

A4012

Hockley Ct

Birch's Close

Kilby Rd

PO

The Blackbirds

Works

Travelodge

Little Lane

Hockcliffe Business Centre

Hockcliffe House

Bull Farm

Field Farm

5

26

LEIGHTON ROAD

496

A B **30** C D

1 grid square represents 500 metres

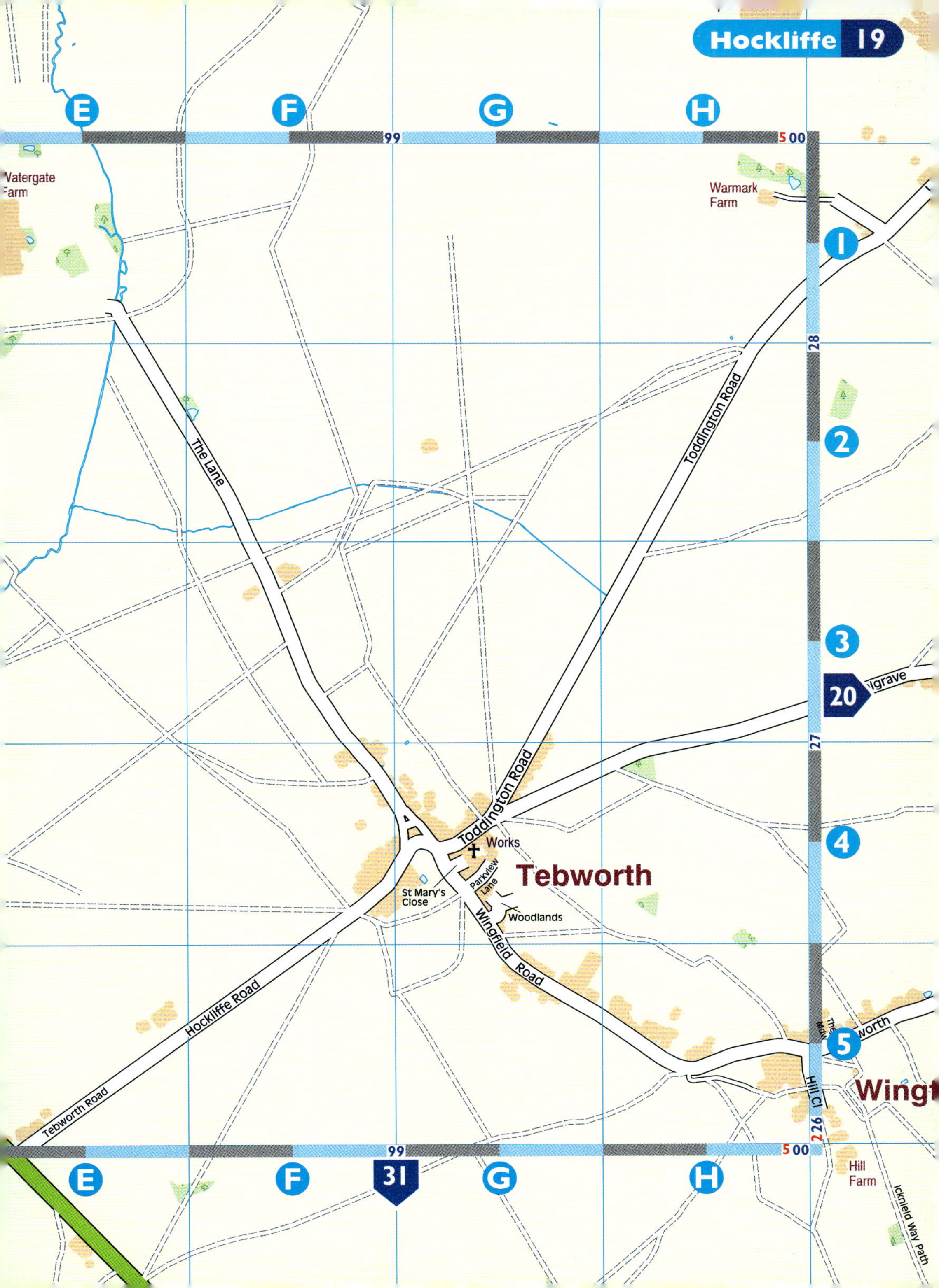

E   F   G   H

99   500

Watergate
Farm

Warmark
Farm

I

28

The Lane

Toddington Road

2

3

20 Igrave

27

Toddington Road

4

Works

Tebworth

Parkview Lane

St Mary's
Close

Woodlands

Wingfield Road

Hockliffe Road

The M...

worth

5

Wingf

Tebworth Road

Hill Cl

26

99   500

E   F   31   G   H

Hill
Farm

Icknield Way Path

A B **10** C **TODINGTON** D

I

Warmark Farm

Alma Farm
C P Sch
England
Health Clinic
Mander La
Wentworth Gdns
SPI
Mr PI

Leighton Road
Meadow Rd
Russell Road
Chapel CI
Craw Gdns
Toddington Medical Centre
The Crs
Luton Rd
Path
Way

28

Bryant WY
Stockdale
Dale
Lakefield AV
Princes Street
Bush CI

Rose Wk
The Cleavers
Preston Rd
Bradford Rd

Willow Way
Randall Drive
Bradford WY
Kimberwell
Bradford Road

Luton Road

LU

Fancott

2

Shelton AV
Mount Pleasant Avenue

A5120

Dropsholt Farm

Icknield
Way
Path

Chalgrave Manor
New Barn Far

3

19

27

Chalgrave Road
ROAD

Chalgrave

4

Icknield Way Path
DUNSTABLE
Chalgrave Manor Golf Club
Golf Course

5

The Mdw
Tebworth Road
New Barn Farm Lane

Hill CI
Wingfield
226

Grove Farm

5 00
A B **32** C D

Hill Farm

Icknield Way

LORDS

1 grid square represents 500 metres

B530

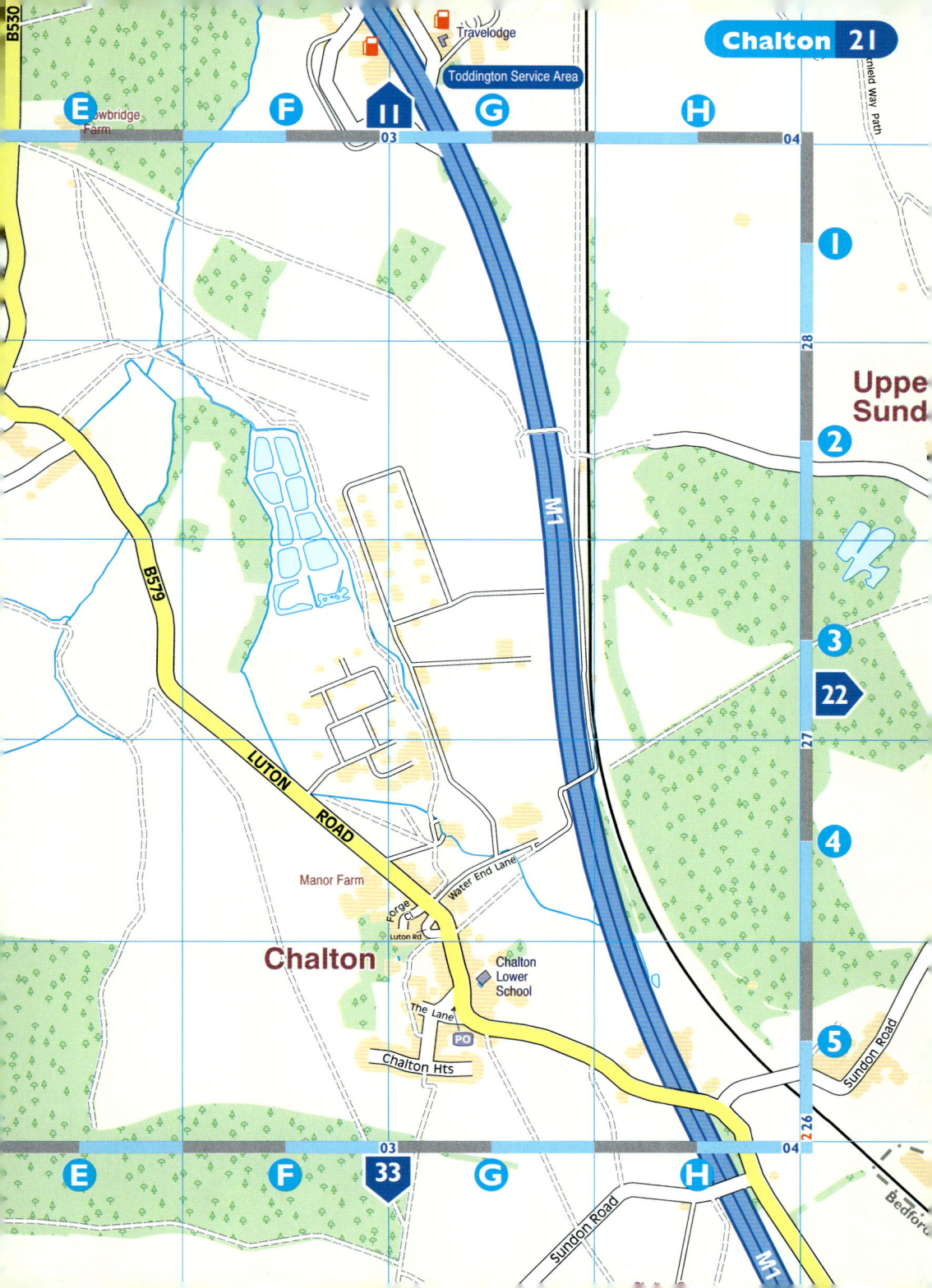

E owbridge Farm
F
H

Travelodge
Toddington Service Area
G

I

Uppe
Sund

2

22
3

Manor Farm

LUTON ROAD

B579

M1

Water End Lane

Forge Cl
Luton Rd

Chalton

Chalton Lower School

The Lane
PO
Chalton Hts

4

5

Sundon Road

Bedfor

E
F
33
G
H

Sundon Road

M1

A B **I2** C D
05

 Icknield Way Path

Icknield Way

Harlington Road

Icknield Way Path

Holtwood Farm

I

28

Upper Sundon

Harlington Rd

Common

La
Slate
Hall

Hills Vw

Sundon Lower School

Streatley Road

Manor Road

2

Church Road

3

21

27

Lower Sundon

Manor Road

4

Manor Farm

Sundon Road

5

Sundon Road

2 26

M1

Luton Bedfordshire Court

Pinewood Cl

Chestnut Way

Sycmr Cl

Epping Way

Lilac Cv

Lime Tree Close

Mendip Way

Arbroath Rd

Kinmoor

Crescent

Brussels Way

Firbank Cl

05

A B **34** C D

Camford Wy

Camford

Sundon Business Park

Dencora Wy

Sundon Industrial Est

Willowgate Trading Estate

Graham

Welifield Av

Oakwood Drive

Ashwell

Engate

Redwood Dr

Sundon Park Junior School

Way

Atholl Cl

Kinross

Galst

Rossfold

Cranbrook Drh

Alpine Way

Road

Ranock Cl

Close

uplands

E F 13 G H

Church Road

St Mary's Cl

Chu 07

Stanley Rd

Stanley

Streatley Road

Sundon Road

Streatley

Bury La

Sharpenhoe Road

Sharpenhoe Rd

Icknield Way Path

Luton Road A6

I

28

2

60

John Bunyan Trail

BARTON

ROAD

George Wood

3

New Farm

24

27

4

John Bunyan Trail

Great Bramingham Lane

Great Bramingham Farm

Hayton Cl

Skelton Close

Gthla

Gdns

Gdns

Dalton Cl

Rise

Turnpike Dr

Bramingham

Whitehaven

LU3

Whitehorse Vale

Burford Cl

Catesby Gn

Woodmere

Quennock

Launton Cl

Milburn Cl

Statham

Holford Wy

Turnpike Dr

BARTON ROAD

Underwood

Cl

Olympic

Northwell

Winchester Gdns

shire Way

Dr

Petersfield Gdns

Denmark Cl

Whitehorse Vale

Mees Cl

Harleston Cl

Sworder Cl

Kirby

Albury

Ames Cl

Arbour Cl

Fernham

Gdns

Charndon

Cl

Elvington Gdns

Edgcott Cl

Scombe Gn

prcrft

Chard Drive

Dexter

Binns

2 26

Cardi

Newr

Seco

Enterprise Wy

E F 35 G H

Kholm Way

Northwell Drive

Denham Close

Brompton

Great Bramingham Wood

Lea Manor Recreation Centre

Lea Manor High School

Whitefield Junior School

Morris

Carnegie Gdns

Drive

Gilder Cl

Oregon Wy

Silver Birch Wy

Celandine

Silverberry Cl

Cicero Dr

Campania

Freeman Av

Surg

Bramingham Primary School

Superstore

Barnfield College Technology Centre

Bramingham Park Study Centre

Whitwell Cl

Spayne

Superstore

Bramingham Business Park

Markh

Lncstr

Allendale

A   B   **14**   C   Barton Hill Farm   D

5 08   09

I

John Bunyan Trail

28

Icknield Way Path

Hertfordshire County
Bedfordshire County

2

60

BARTON

3

New
Farm

Icknield   Way   Path
Icknield Way Path

23

27

John Bunyan Trail

ROAD

4

Golf Course

John Bunyan Trail

John Bunyan Trail
ingham Lane

South Bedfordshire
Golf Club

5

Quantock Cl
Rise
Statham Cl
Milburn Cl
Elvington Gdns
d Wy
Chard Drive
B'm wd
Dexter
S'combe
Sprcrftl

Turnpike Dr
Turnpike Dr
Turnpike
Dr

Danyers Dr
Farrow
BARTON ROAD

Icknield Way Path

26
5 08 Wy

Cardinal
Newman Catholic
Secondary School

A   Warden Hill Rd   B   **36**   C   D

09

Superstore

Enter
Barnfield College
Technology Centre

Bramingham
Business
Park

Chapel Cl
Warden Hill Gdns
Lncstr Av

Quantock
Cl

Whitwell Cl
Spayne

1 grid square represents 500 metres

E F 15 G H

I

Mortgrove
Farm

John Bunyan Trail

Lilley
Hoo

28

2

Hexton Road

Lilley Manor
Farm

Pond Farm

Ward's
Farm

Hexton Road

3

26

Rectory
La

Lilley

27

Ward's Wood

John Bunyan Trail

Gn
Acres

Dell

4

John Bunyan Trail

Rueley
Road

East Street

The Baulk

Hertfordshire County
Bedfordshire County

Lilley
Wood

West Street

5

Lilley Bottom

226

E F 37 G H

HILL

A505

Dog Kennel
Farm

A   B   **Little Offley** C   D

5 12   13

I

28

Lilley Hoo

2

Cloudshill

Westend F

3

25

Lilley Hoo Farm

27

A505

Lilley

Gn
Acres

Lilleyhoo Lane

Luton Road

Rueley
Road

4

The Baulk

East Street

Hollybush Hill

Luton White Hill

West Street

5

Lilley Bottom

2 26

5 12   13

A   B   **38**   C   D

A505

HILL

Dog Kennel
Farm

Luton White Hill

*Westbu
Wood*

1 grid square represents 500 metres

E F G H

15 16

I

Offley
Grange

A505

2

28

Hill

Offley

School Lane

Offley Endowed
Primary School

3

Offley
Place

27

High Street

Road

Great
Offley

West
Lane

Gosling
Av

King's

Lawns
Cl

Clarion
Cl

Salusbury Lane

Salusbury
La

4

Harris Lane

Harris Lane

Walden

Road

5

Offley
Hoo

226

West
Wood

E F G H

15 39 16

A B 16 C D

I

Stoke Road
Globe Lane
PH Grand Union
Works
The Martins Drive

Buckin...
Bedfor...
Valley Farm
26
490
91

Chestnut Rise
Milebush
Soulbury Road
Chestnut Hill
Alwins Field
Knaves Hill
Knaves Hill
Rowley
Furrows
Uppr Cmb
Uncombe Slade
Rothschild Road
Bossington Lane
Works
Cou...
Buil...
Princes...

Cleveland Drive
Malvern Dr
Biderford Green
Cotswold
Biderford Green
Biderford Gn
Derwent Road
Fyne
Loyne Cl
Lochy Dr
Corbet Ride
St Mary's Way
Hawthorne Close
Beech Grove
Soulbury Rd
Golden Riddy
Lime Gv
30
The Paddocks
Harcourt
Stoke Road
Faulkner's Way
Vimy Road
Surgery
Millbow
Millstream Ct
Clinic
Windsor Av

Greenleas Lower School
Drive
Maree
Carron
Nevis Cl
Lomond Dr
Morar Gdns
Delamere Gdns
Rannock Gardens
W Gdns
Lochy Drive
Coniston Road
Southcott Lower Sch
Mowbray Dr
Linslade Lower School
Grasmere Wy
Works
Roseberry Av
Durrell Cl
Superstore
The Mary Bass Lower School
Water La
West

Derwent
255
Erribol Cl
Leven Cl
Bewdley
Melfort Dr
Blakedown
Melfort Dr
Ullswater Dr
Linslade
Hanover Ct
Kendal
Grasmere Way
Rock Lane
Rock Cl
Shnert Lane
Leighton Road
Springfield Rd
New Road
PO
Old Rd
Hills Ct
Leighton Rd
Friday
Brdg St
Judges
La

Himley Green
Ascot Dr
Apple Tree Cl
Southcourt Av
Brnbs
Grange Close
Leighton Buzzard Station
Station Rd
Vcrg Rd
Church Road
SM Rd
Works
Surgery

Chelsea Green
Chelsea Green
Epsom Cl
Bunkers Lane
Village Court
Woodside Wy
Orchard Dr
Waterloo Road
Vicarage Gdns
Victoria
The Gables
Wing Road
Memorial Park
Mardle Road
Grand Union Canal Walk
Two Ridges Link
Pulfor...
Lowe...

Southcott Village
Wyngates
Stephenson Close
Wyngates
Cedars Way
Finch Crs
Ledburn Gv
Ashcumm Crs
Mentmore Road
Camberton Road

4
490
224

Wing Road
Mentmore Gdns
Mentmore Road
Tiddenfoot Leisure Centre
Linslade Middle Sch
The Cedars Upper Sch & Comm Coll
Grovebury Road Industrial Estate

A4146
WING ROAD
5

LU7

A505

Grand Union Canal
River Ouzel

A B C D

LEIGHTON BUZZARD

Leedon

Vandyke Upper School & Comm Co...
Gilbert Inglefield Middle School
Beaudesert Lower School
St Georges Lower School
Cemetery
Clipstone Brook Industrial Estate
Clipstone Brook Lower Sch
Stratton Brook Mews
Brooklands Middle School
Leedon Lower School
Youngs Industrial Est
Cherrycourt Way Industrial Estate
Stanbridge Road
Comm Indus...
Adastral Av
Billington P...
Leighton Buzzard Railway
Page's Park Station
Page's Park
Leighton Town FC Sports Ground
Council Building
Fire Station
Leighton Buzzard Theatre Cinema
Superstore
Chiltern Trading Est
Pages Ind Pk
Leighton Ind Park
Harmill Industrial Estate
Industrial Estate
Spinney Park Industrial Estate
Grovebury Farm
Johnson Drive
Wayside Farm House

Churchill Road
Tindall Av
Nelson Road
Nelson Road
Hornbeam
Greenlands
Meadway
Appenine
Phoenix Cl
Hydrus Dr
Jupiter Dr
Mercury Way
Aquila Rd
Orion Way
Lyra Gdns
Gemini Close
Saturn Rd
Columba Dr
Willow Bank Wk
Dove Tree Rd
Almond Rd
Clarence Road
Roosevelt Av
Pennyvale
Ash Gv
Garden Hedge
East St
Pear Tree La
Plum Tree La
East St
St Georges Close
Summer Street
Vandyke Road
Regent Street
George St
Miles Avenue
Atterbury Avenue
Brook Street
Brookside Wk
Kiteleys Gn
Middle Gn
Carina Drive
Pegasus Ct
Cetus
N Star
Nebular Way
Omega Rd
Centauri Cl
Neptune Gdns
Hockliffe Road
A4012
HOCKLIFFE ROAD
Capshill Av
Waterdell
Leedon Furlong
Fallowfield Cl
Clipstone Crs
Midway
Russell Way
Hinton Cl
Saxons Cl
Danes Way
Meadow Way
Meadow Way
Meadow Way
Mllrs
Wheatfield Cl
Rye Way
Woodman Cl
Albany Road
Lovent Dr
Cutlers Way
South Street
Brooklands
Garden Leys
Brooklands
Highfield Road
Highfield Road
Crossway
Marley Flds
Marley Flds
Greaves Way
Cherrycourt Way
Acacia Cl
Stanbridge Road
Ind Est
Richmond Road
Highcroft
Weston Av
The Chilterns
Bc Cl
Bc Cl
Stanbridge Road
Lydd Wy
Harmony Row
Concord Way
Harrow Road
Weston Road
Richmond Rd
The Vyne
Nettleton Cl
New Weston Roundel
Driveway
Esmonde
Swales Dr
Liddell Wy
Adastral Av
Groovebury Road
Billington Road
The Maltings
Linwood Gv
Stansbridge Red Terr
Chaloner Ct
Cooper
Ridgeley E & W Dr
Avery Cl
Furlong
Reeves Cl
Gibson Dr
Warnerford
Mamock Dr
Hawker Dr
Nicholl Dr
Nicolson Drive
Midleton Way
Palmer Cres
Draper Way
Goodman Rd
Carlside
Dwill Cl
Bushell Rd
Works
Johnson Drive
Garland Way
Reeves Cl
Byford Path
Cormorant Wy
Sandpiper Way
Turnham Dr
Moorhouse
Middleton Way
Ash Cra
Eden Way
Ind Est
Firbank Way
Charmoor Road
Enterprise Way
Boss Av
Chartmoor Road
Grovebury Road
A505
A505
A41

Lake St
HCKLFF ST
Surg
Church Street
Baker St
Bedford St
North St
Lammas Walk
Bossard Ct
Grove Road
Duncombe Dr
Lindler
Beaudesert
Pol Stn
Mag Cl

LEIGHTON ROAD

Centre

Hockliffe
House

Bull
Farm

A
B
18
C
D

Lane

496
26
97

I

2
25

Mill Road

3

Tilsworth

Warren
Knoll

Bury Rise

Blackhill

High
Banks

Stanbridge
Lower School

Kings Way

Stanbridge Road

Mill Road

4

Stanbridge

Tilsworth Road

Laurel Cl

Orchard Way

Green Cl

Lords Cl

Manor
Farm

Leighton Road

St
Johns
Cl

Beacon
VW

224

PH

Peddars Lane

Station Road

Bluegate
Farm

5

496
97

A
B
40
C
D

Stanbridgeford

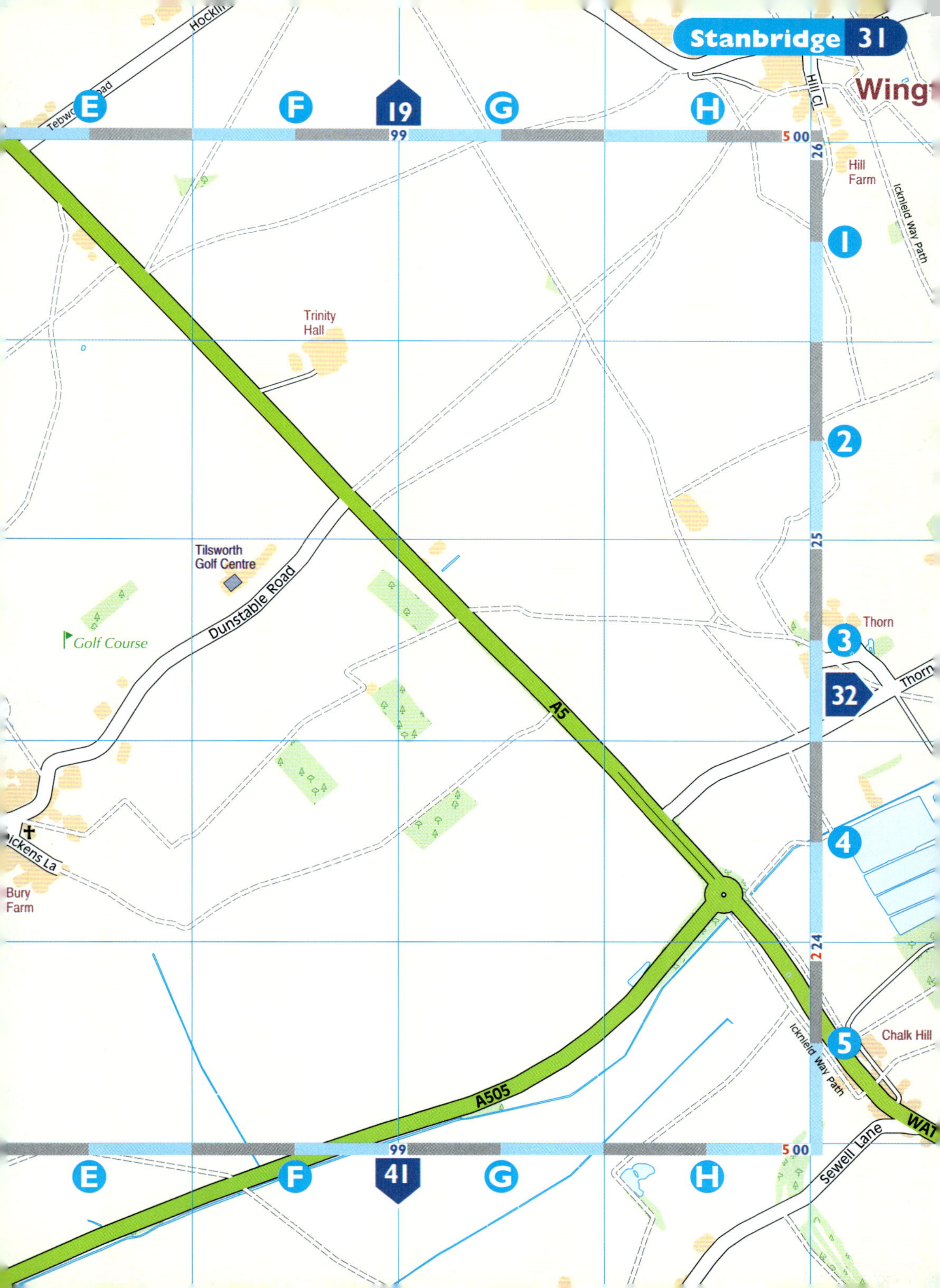

Wing

E F **19** G H
99
5 00
26

Hill
Farm

Ickneild Way Path

I

Trinity
Hall

2

25

Tilsworth
Golf Centre

Dunstable Road

Thorn

3

Golf Course

32

Thorn

A5

4

ⴕckens La

2 24

Bury
Farm

Ickneild Way Path

Chalk Hill

5

A505

Sewell Lane

WA

E F **41** G H
99
5 00

32

Tebworth
The Mdw
Hill Cl

Wingfield

(A) (B) LORD'S HILL **20** (C) Grove Farm (D)
01

26 5 00

Hill Farm

Icknield Way Path

(I)

25

A5120

(2)

Thorn Road

Dunstablians RUFC

Bidwell

(3)

Thorn

Thorn Road

Icknield Way Path

BEDFORD

Tithe Farm Lower School

31

Tithe Farm
Long Cl
Dell Rd
Tithe
Mdw

ROAD

Bankside Cl

Plaiters Wy

Roslyn Way

Churchfield Road

Delmont Rd

All Saints

(4)

Icknield Way Path

Bidwell Hil

Bryel Wy

Thomas Whitehead CE School

Health Cen

2 24

Coopers Way

St Michaels Av

Watling Rd

Roman Gdns

High

Houghton Regis Lower School

Mill Rd

Arnald Wy

HIGH STREET

Cprs Wy

Queen St

Dunstable Rd

(5)

Icknield Way Path

Chalk Hill

Millers Way

Farers Wy

Millers Wy

Millers

Houghton Regis Trading Centre

Cem

Townsend Industrial Estate

Cemetery

Portland Rd

Man

Sewell Lane

WATLING

40

STREET

A5

5 00

(A) (B) **42** (C) (D)
01

HOUGHTON ROAD

Townsend Farm Rd

Blackburn Road

West Orchard

Mayer

Circle Business

Ivinghoe Business

The Northfields Technology

I grid square represents 500 metres

E   F   21   G   H

03

I

Chalton Hts

PO

ne Lane

Sundon Road

M1

Chalton Cross Farm

Bedfo

26

2

Thornhill Lower School

Thornbury Court

Grove Rd

Grove Rd

Thornhill Cl

Grove Rd

Yew St

Hillborough Crescent

Eddiwick Av

Kent Road

Sundon Road

Kings Houghton Middle School

Melton Walk

Abbey Walk

Maple Way

Rose Walk

Therfield Walk

Ashwell Walk

Houghton Park Rd

25

3

34

Tithe Farm

Road

Sycamore Road

Black Thorn Rd

Farm Rd

Recreation Road

Westminster Gdns

Parkside Drive

PO

Briarwood

Parkside Drive

Elm Pk Cl

Enfield Cl

Trident Drive

Dolphin Drive

Hinton Walk

Newbury Rd

Parkside Drive

Cumbria Cl

Fensome Dr

Conquest Rd

Fenwick Rd

Henley Rd

Rosedale

Conway

Leafields

Leafields Cl

Easthill Road

Dalling Farm Cl

Hammersmith Gdns

Lower School

Parkside

Chelsea Gdns

Hawthorn Park Lower School

Bromley Gardens

Turner

Vanbrugh

Constable

Nash Cl

Bridgman

Lowry Drive

Stubbs

Bloomsbury Gdns

4

Crossways

Windsor Dr

Parks de Cl

edical Cen

East End

The Green

Woodlands Av

Lombrooke

Brookfield

Park Av

Kingsland Cl

Houghton Regis

Surgery

Pastures Wy

Paddock

Gelding Cl

Thresher

St Kilda Rd

Sussex Cl

Peregrine Road

Kestrel

Skua

Lapwing

Bunting Rd

Linn

Swallow

2 24

5

arkes Way

Moore Crs

Windsor Road

Hailey's Wy

Tennyson Av

Milton Wy

North

Evans Cl

Copperfields

Kensington

Tudor Drive

Sandringham Dr

Wheatfield Cl

Plough Binder

Landrace Road

Reaper

Haymarket

PO

Thatch

Radnor Road

Oatfield Cl

Thurlow

Tomlinson

Chantry J&I School

Lewsey Fm Clinic

Wedgwood Rd

Southfi Infant School

Beadlow Road

Purcell Rd

Life Cl

Trefoil

Clover

Santoin

Pastures

Roy Cl

St M

Houghton Hall

Regis Road

Marlin Rd

Kimberley

Cartax Cl

Brunel Cl

Apsley

Belsize Rd

Abercorn

Aldaido

Lewsey Fa

Drayton Av

Friesian Cl

Jersey Cl

Guernsey

Hereford Rd

Percheron Cl

E   F   43   G   H

03

Foster

Woodside Park Industrial Estate

woodside

Porz Avenue

Humphrys Road

Poynters Rd

Kirkwood Road

Rodney

High

Street

Braintree

Ann

Percheron

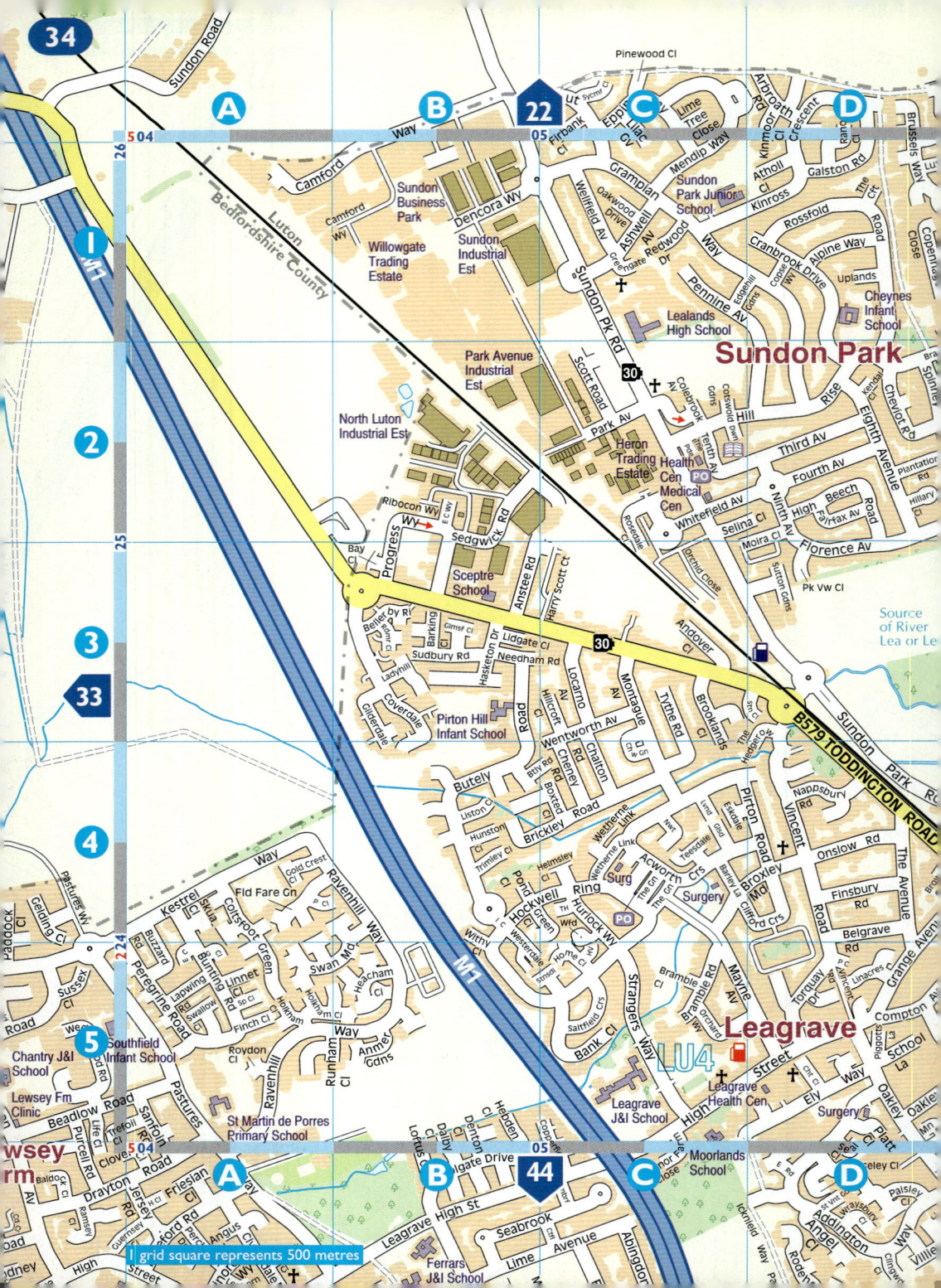

Sundon Park

Leagrave

Pinewood Cl

Sundon Road

Sundon Business Park

Willowgate Trading Estate

Sundon Industrial Est

Dencora Wy

Camford Way

Camford

Grampian

Sundon Park Junior School

Mendip Way

Firbank Cl

Epping Cl

Lilac Gv

Lime Tree Close

Arbroath Rd

Kinmoor Crescent

Atholl

Galston Rd

Brussels Way

Oakwood Drive

Ashwell Av

Greengate

Redwood Dr

Kinross

Rossfold Rd

Cranbrook Drive

Alpine Way

Uplands

Cheynes Infant School

Copenhill

Bedfordshire County

Luton

Wellfield Av

Sundon Pk Rd

Lealands High School

Pennine Av

Edgehill Gdns

Cotswold Dns

Colebrook

Hill

Rise

Eighth Avenue

Cheviot Rd

Kendal

North Luton Industrial Est

Park Avenue Industrial Est

Scott Road

Park Av

Heron Trading Estate

Health Cen

Medical Cen

Whitefield Av

Third Av

Fourth Av

Ninth Av

High

Beech

Fairfax Av

Plantation Rd

Hillary

Florence Av

Ribocon Wy

Progress Wy

EC Wy

Sedgwick Rd

Bay Cl

Sceptre School

Anstee Rd

Harry Scott Ct

Selina Cl

Moira Ct

Lorenta Close

Sutton Gdns

Pk Vw Cl

Source of River Lea or Le

Bellow by Rd

Barking

Glmsf Cl

Lidgate Cl

Needham Rd

Andover Cl

Sudbury Rd

Hasketon Dr

Ladyhill

Coverdale

Gillerdale

Pirton Hill Infant School

Road

Hillcroft

Locarno

Montague

Av

Tythe Rd

Brooklands

The

Butely

Liston Cl

Hunston Cl

Trimley Cl

Brickley

Wentworth Av

Chalton

Cheney

Road

Boxted

Wetherne

Nappsbury Rd

Pirton Road

Vincent

Onslow Rd

The Avenue

Finsbury Rd

Helmsley

Pond Green

Acworth Crs

Surgery

Lynet

Eskdale

Broxley Rd

Clifford Crs

Belgrave Rd

Hockwell Ring

Hurlock Wy

Wd

PO

Saltfield Crs

Bank Rd

Bramble Rd

Orchard

Mayne Av

Torquay Rd

Grange Avenue

Compton Av

Piggotts

School La

Withy

Strangers Way

LU4

Leagrave High Street

Leagrave Health Cen

Ely

Surgery

Oakley

Platt

Chantry J&I School

Southfield Infant School

Lewsey Fm Clinic

Kestrel

Skua

Colstpoot Green

Bunting Rd

Linnet

Swallow

Ravenhill Way

Swan Mead

Heacham Cl

Finch Cl

Hokham

Gold Crest

Fld Fare Gn

Peregrine Road

Lapwing

Buzzard

Roydon Cl

Runham Cl

Anmer Gdns

Sussex Rd

Gelding Cl

Paddock Cl

Pastures Wy

Beadlow Rd

Purcell Rd

Sanford Rd

Trefoil

Clover

St Martin de Porres Primary School

Pastures

Friesian Rd

Jersey Rd

Guernsey Rd

Drayton Rd

Angus

Ramsey

Leagrave High St

Seabrook

Lime Avenue

Dalby Cl

Denton Rd

Lochgate Drive

Hebden Rd

Copeland

Leagrave J&I School

Moorlands School

Addington Way

Paisley Cl

B579 TODDINGTON ROAD

Sundon Park

M1

1 grid square represents 500 metres

Marsh Farm

Limbury

Great Bramingham Wood

Lea Manor Recreation Centre
Lea Manor High School
Woodlands Secondary School
Whitefield Junior School
Waulud Primary School
The Meads Primary School
Bramingham Primary School
Barnfield College Technology Centre
Bramingham Park Study Centre
Bramingham Business Park
Superstore
Superstore
Medical Cen
Gooseberry Hill Health Cen
Warden Hill Infant School
Warden Hill Junior School
Icknield High School
Icknield Primary School
William Austin Infant School
William Austin Junior School
Beechwood Primary Sch
Norton Road Primary School
St Josephs Infant School
Surgery

Whitehorse Vale
Northwell Drive
Brompton Close
Bramingham Road
Ailsworth Road
Homerton Road
Calverton Road
Bosmore Rd
Icknield Way Path
Willow Way
River Wy
Hurst Way
Westmorland Road
Limbury Road
Icknield Road
Marsh Road
Wickstead Road
Pembroke Avenue
Roman Road
Grasmere Road
Dewsbury Rd
Birdsfoot Lane
Catherall
Catsbrook Road
Grosvenor Road
Riverside Rd
Neville Road
Bristol Road
Trinity Road
St Ethelbert Avenue
St Augustine Avenue
Fallowfield
Rackman Lane
Leagrave Road
B579
Cuffley Av

E F 23 G H
I
2
3 36
4
5
E F 45 G H

A   B   **24**   C   D
09

Chatham
Turnpike Dr
Danvers Dr
Elwington Gdns
Ford Way
Darrow
Chard Drive
Binscombe Av

Ickneild Way Path

Cardinal
Newman Catholic
Secondary School

Quantock
Barnfield College
Technology Centre
Whitwell Cl
Spavne
Cl
Marsom
Gn
Sples Cl
Gdns

Enterprise Wy
Superstore
Bramingham
Business
Park
I

Chapel Rd
Warden Hill Rd
Warden Hi
Gdns
Lncstr Av
Warden Hl

Links Wy

Markham
Rd
Wycombe Wy
Hillcrest
Av
Ickneild Way
Poplar Av

Ickneild Way Path

Grasmere Road
Grasmere
Av
Derwent Av
Welbury
Av

Hillview Crs
Kelling
Weybourne
Dr
Wiveton
Cl
Langham
Cl
Blakeney

Cromer
Furze
Cl
Farmbrook

The Furrows
Gooseberry
Gooseberry Hill
Health Cen
Laburn
Grove
Laburnum
Close
Claydon Rd

Warden
Hill Infant
School
Warden Hill
Junior School
Birdsfoot Lane
Enderby Rd
Springfield Rd

Bckhm
Binham
Wisng Cl
Thornage

Wn
Langdown

Ickenild Dovedate
The
Belfry

Luton

2

Marfton
Halyard
Rd
Wodecroft Road
Avon Rd
Wycliffe
Rd
Levpoume

Glenfield Rd

Old
Bedford
Rd
Winton Cl
Foxbury
Cl
Ringwood
Cl

Bedford   Road

Cromer   Way
Lorrimer Cl
The
Magpies

Hancock
Lambourn
Kestrel Wy

Bedfordshire Cou

3
35
PO
DR

East Hill
Birdsfoot Lane
Dewsbu

Sherborne Rd
Egdon Dr
Blandford Av
Hemingford
Dr

Old Bedford Road

John Dony
Field Cen
V
Prestwick Cl
Gleneagles Dr
Muirfield

Ickneild Primary
School
Icknield High
School
Rackman
Dr
Rosslyn
Crescent

Barnfield Avenue

Pomeroy Gv
Kidne
Pomeroy
Heron Dr
Kilmarnock Dr
Hawkfields

4
Riddy
Truvedns
Truro
Gdns
Lane
Broughton
Holmbrook

Barnfield
College

Medical
Centre
Bushmead Rd
Robinswood

Foxhill
S Hanks
Benington Cl

Stops
Comm

Numery
Carol
Moat Lane
Reeves
Av
Meadow
Rd
Lucerne

Midhurst Gdns
New Bedford Road
Bideford
Gdns

Kingsdown Avenue
Stratton
Gdns
Avebury
Av
Marston Gardens

Bushmead
Primary
School

Bushmead   Road

Luton
Sixth Form
College

Lippitts
Hl

Fairford Avenue

5
Austin
Fallowfield
William
Austin
Infant
School
Winslow
Cl
Wadnurst
Avenue
Graham
Gdns

Westlecote
Gdns
Manton

Bradgers   Hill

Honeygate

Road
Stopsley
High School

Galliard
William Austin
Junior School
Culverhouse
St Ethelbert Avenue

River Lea of Lee

Knoll Rd

Wychwood Avenue

A   B   **46**   C   D
09

St Margarets Av
St Catherines Av
St Winifreds Av
St Lawrences Av
Mildreds Rd
Fountains Road

St Michael's Crs

Priory
Dr
Greenhill
Av

Elmwood Crs
Chartwell
Gn
Birchen
Acorn Cl
Virginia
Sunset Cl
Fair Oak
Sunningfd

St Monicas
Avenue
St Augustine Avenue
Cranleigh Gardens
PO

Montrose   Avenue
30
A5228 STOCKINGSTONE

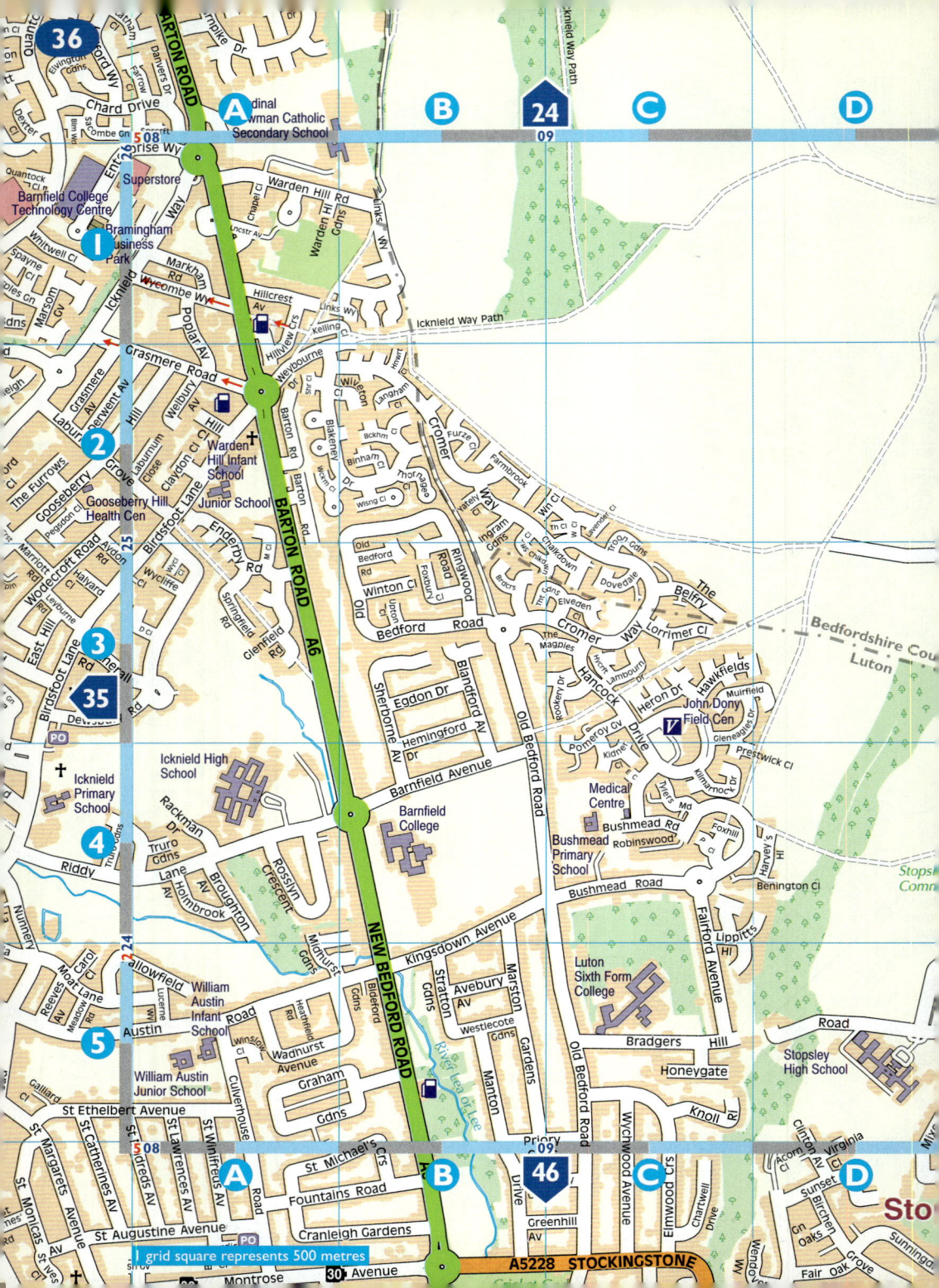

I grid square represents 500 metres

Sto

E   F   **25**   G   H

Wood

Lilley Bottom

A505

Dog Kennel Farm

I

BEECH HILL

Whitehill Farm

Bedfordshire County
Luton

Butterfield Gn Rd

2

26

25

Butterfield Green

HITCHIN RD

Putteridge Bury

University of Bedfordshire

3

38

Butterfield Green

The Vale Crematorium

The Vale Cemetery

A505

Manor Farm

Wren Close

Nightingale Cl

Jaywood

Edgewood Drive

Mount Grace Rd

Curlew

Corncrake Close

Putteridge High School

4

Putteridge Rd

40

Swifts Green Road

Wood Green Road

Ravenbank Road

Crowland Road

Recreation Centre

HITCHIN ROAD

HITCHIN Rd

Wood Gn Cl

Swifts Gn

Putteridge J&I Sch

Rogate Rd

Bkgrv Cl

Birling Rd

Slcmb Cl

Pvns Cl

Ambr Cl

Middl Rd

24

Stopsley Sports Centre
Sports Ground

Cannon Lane

Greenways

Mullion Cl

Delicot Cl

El Ct

Putteridge

Hayes Road

Chesford Road

Rochester Av

Westway

Selsey Drive

F E C

Lothair Road

Venetia

Tancred Rd

Hawthorn Avenue

Stapleford Road

Applecroft Rd

Briar Cl

Blackthorn Dr

Wandon Close

5

Cockernhoe

St Thomas's Rd

St Ths Cl

Ch Rd

PO

Surgery

Hazelwood Close

Mayflld Rd

Ravensthorpe

Peartree Road

Green Lane

Chesford Rd

Eastfield Cl

Saldean

Wandon Way

Telscombe Way

Stopsley Primary School

Ashcroft Rd

Walnut Cl

Dahlia Cl

Wigmore Lane

Plplars

Sowerby Av

Telscombe Way

Brackesham Gdns

A505

Hitchin

STOPSLEY WAY

Sheldon Way

Forrest Crs

Langford

Sacred Heart Primary School

Surgery

Brays Road

Hallwicks Rd

Mobley Gn

Lt Church St

Rck Cl

Lady Zia

Garretts M

Long Lane

Lullington Cl

Alfriston Close

Seaford Cl

Telscombe Wy

Ilford Cl

Hayling Drive

Nymans Rd

Coptho

Elmtre

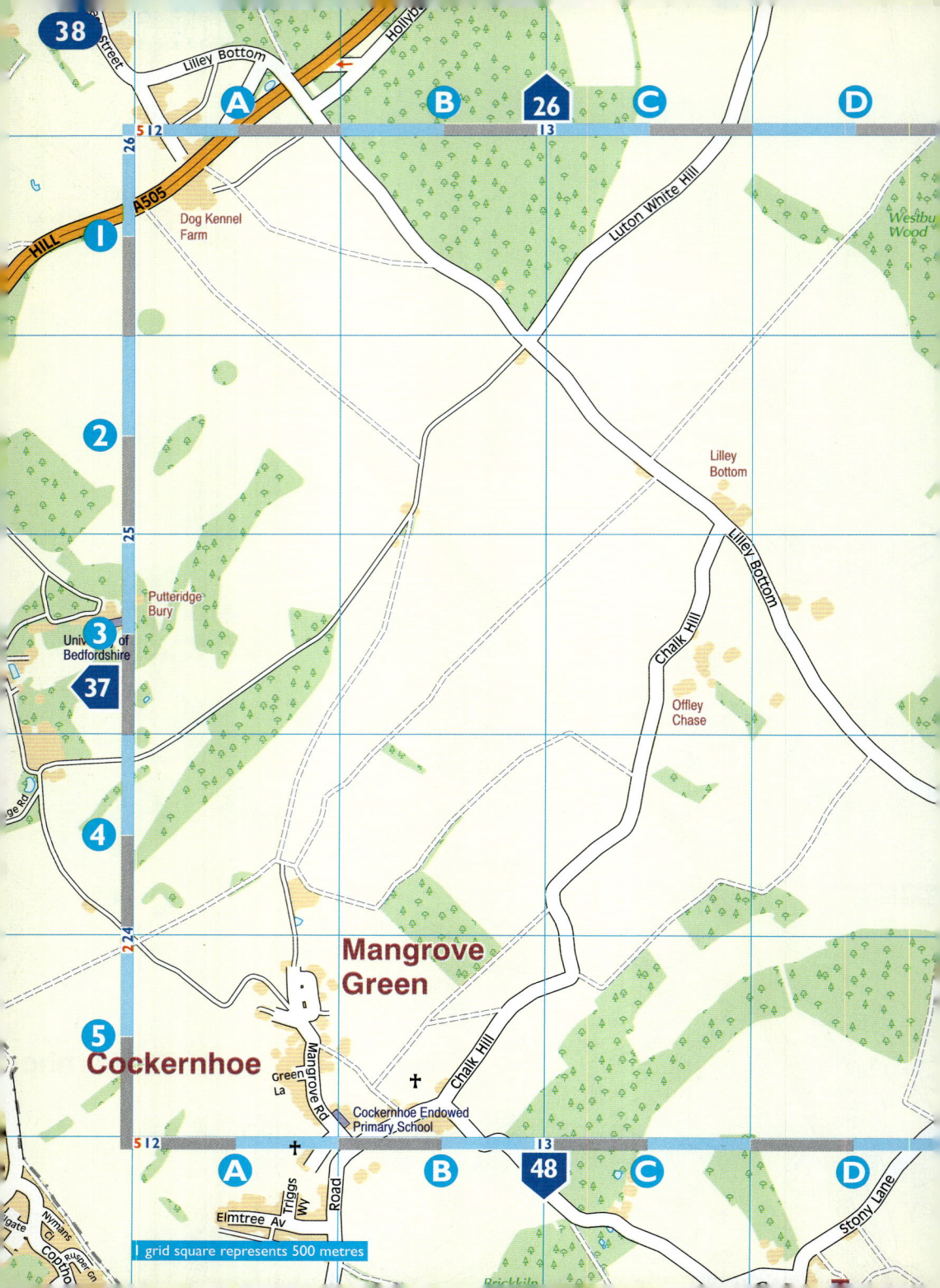

38

Lilley Bottom

A

B

26

C

D

5 12

26

HILL

A505

I

Dog Kennel Farm

Luton White Hill

Westbu Wood

Lilley Bottom

2

25

Putteridge Bury

3

University of Bedfordshire

37

Chalk Hill

Lilley Bottom

Offley Chase

4

ge Rd

2 24

Mangrove Green

5

Cockernhoe

Mangrove Rd

Green La

Chalk Hill

Cockernhoe Endowed Primary School

5 12

13

48

A

B

C

D

Triggs Wy

Road

Elmtree Av

Nymans Cl

Coptho

gate

Stony Lane

Brickkiln

1 grid square represents 500 metres

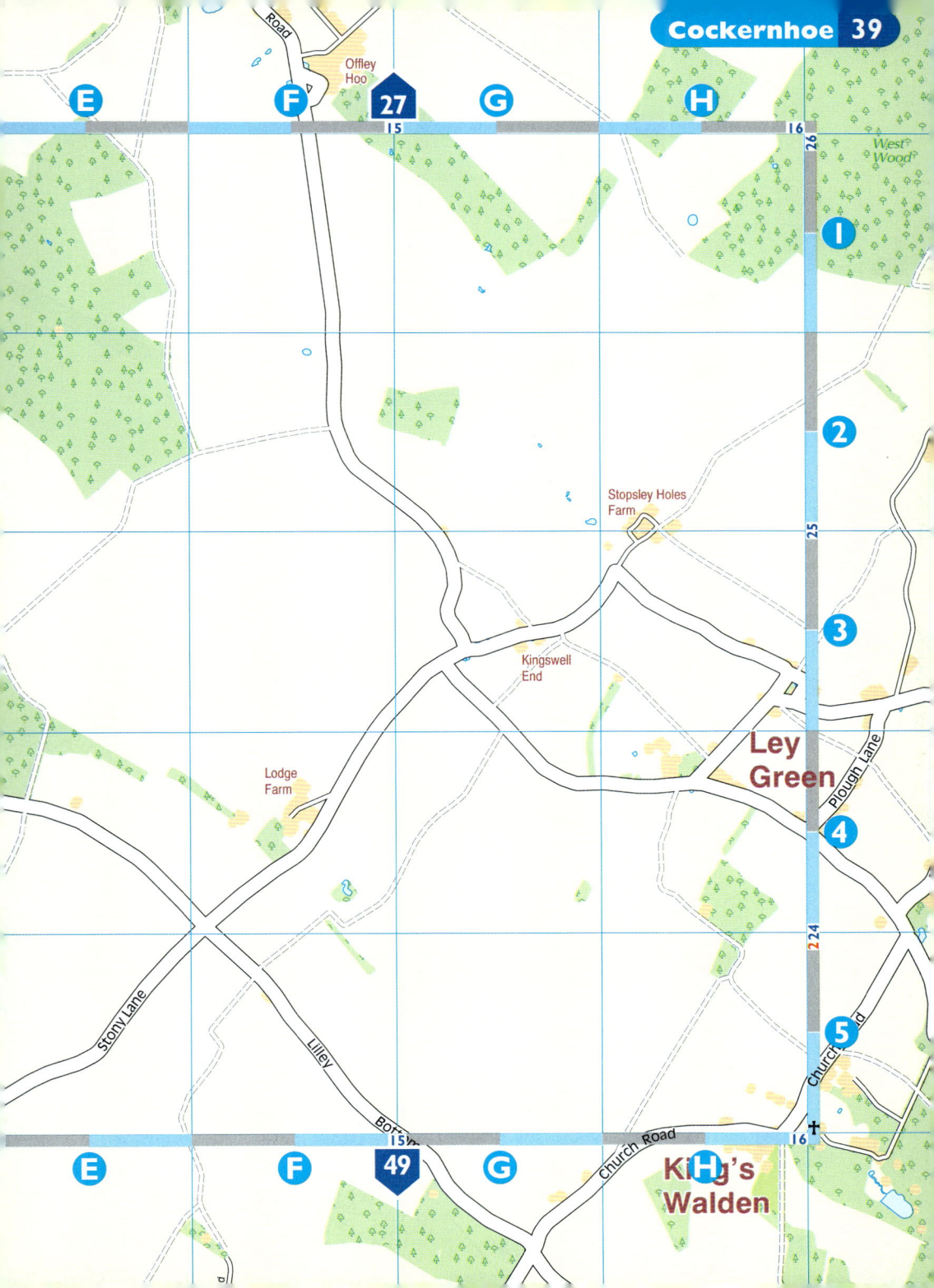

E　**F**　**27**　**G**　**H**

15　16

26

Road

Offley
Hoo

West
Wood

I

2

Stopsley Holes
Farm

25

3

Kingswell
End

**Ley
Green**

Plough Lane

Lodge
Farm

4

2 24

Stony Lane

Lilley

5

Church

E　**F**　**49**　**G**

15½

Bottom

Church Road

Kin**g's
Walden**

H

16

†

A   B   **30**   C   D

4 96   97

Station Road

Bluegate Farm

Stanbridgeford

1

50

A505   50   50

23

Stanbridge Road

Stanbridge Road

Knolls View

Works

2

Lower End

3

22

Eaton Bray Road

Castle Hill Road

Chapel Lane

4

Rye Farm

Honeywick

Honeywick Lane

Totternhoe Road

Eaton Green

Green La

The Rye

Dyers Rd

Works

The Orchards

5

Park Farm

Greenways

22 1

4 96   97

A   B   **50**   C   D

Park Lane

Comp

Comp Gate

Cantilupe Cl

PH

Wallace Dr

The Nurseries

Rose Ct

Eaton Bray Lower School

Northall Cl

Church La

Rd Ct

Northcliffe

Saffron Rl

Wivesfield

School Lane

High

Eaton

grid square represents 500 metres

E   F   **31**   G   H

AE05

I

Way Path

Sewell Lane

WATE

99

5 00

23

Sewell Lane

Sewell

2

3

42

22

Cusworth
Wy
Bryony
Aldens
Cl
Greenfield Cl
Saxo
Weathe
Icknield Way
Sc

4

Brownlow Rd

Castle Cl

Totternhoe Quarry
Nature Reserve

Badgers
Badgers Gate
Badgers

Park
Avenue

Lancotbury

Castle Hill Road

Dunstable Town CC

Dunstable   Road

Harvey Rd

Marina Dr

Gardner's
Cl

Beacon Avenue

Coomb

5

Totternhoe

Totternhoe
FC

Church
Gn

Furlong
Lane

Totternhoe
Lower School

Brightwell
Av

The Avenue

2 21

5 00

E   F   **51**   G   Ellesmere   Well   H

99

The Ride

Church Road

**Church
End**

Head
Ro

B489

TR

Beecroft

Grid references (top): 42 · A · B · 32 · C · D

Grid references (left): I · 2 · 3 · 41 · 4 · 5

Grid references (bottom): A · B · 52 · C · D

Chalk Hill · Coopers Way · Houghton Regis Lower School · HIGH ST · Mill Rd · Queen St · Millers Way · Farmers Wy · Millers Cl · Houghton Regis Trading Centre · Townsend Industrial Estate · Houghton Farm · Westcott Orchard

Icknield Way Path · Sewell Lane · WATLING STREET · A5 · HIGH STREET NORTH · Salters Way · Barley Brow · Cheyne · Palma · Suncote Av · Suncote Cl · French's Av · Avenue · Peppercorn Way · French's Cl

The Northfields Technology College · Northfields · Houghton Road · A5120 · Mayer Wy · Circle Business Centre · Ivinghoe Business Cen · Works · Douglas Crs · Northview Road · Arianne Business Centre · Portland Ride

Works · Lawrence Industrial Estate · Dunstable FC · Brewers Hill Rd · Creasey Drive · Station Road · Tavistock St · Glebe · Caproll Rd · Olma Rd · 30 · Works · Printers Wy · Crabtree Way · Duns Park · Go Bowling · Dunstable Leisure Centre · Grove Theatre · Superstore

Brewers Hill Middle School · Aidbanks · Brewers Hill · Beale Street · Chiltern FM · Waterlow Rd · Clifton Road · Stuart Street · Falcon Cl · George St · Surg · Ashton · Ashton CE VA Middle School · Council Building · Quadrant Shop Cen

Weatherfield School · Beecroft Lower School · Westfield Road · Maldenbower Av · Beech Gn · Radburn · Victoria Street · Edward St · Winfield St · Regent St · Albion St

Beecroft · Hillcroft · Greenfield Cl · Saxon Cl · Norman Wy · Weatherby · Icknield Way Path · Cookfield Cl · Bunhill · Drovers · Loring Road · Beecroft · Croft · Chiltern Road · West Parade · Brook Close · Union St · Princes Street · Police Station · Surg

Spinney Crs · Pascomb Rd · 30 · Wornington Rd · Hambling Pl · Way · Leighton Rd · Sports Ground · Surgery · Lower School · Icknield · Bury St · Friary · Friary Fld

Lancot Drive · Lancot Lower School · Badgers Gate · Badgers Cl · Lancot Av · Oakwell Cl · Franklin Rd · Benning Av · B489 · Long Meadow · Kirby Rd · Recreation Ground · First Avenue · Osborne Rd

Marina Dr · Gardner's Cl · Harvey Rd · Beacon Avenue · Coombe Dr · Coombe Dr · Totternhoe Road · Westdown Gdns · Beechwood · WEST STREET · Pipers Croft · Catchacre · Cemetery · Surgery · Windermere · Keswick · Grasmere · Ennerdale Av · Appleby Gdns · Patterdale

The Avenue · TRING ROAD · WHIPSNADE ROAD · Royce Cl · Royce Rd · Leighton Road · Five Knolls · Meadway · 30 · Spoonbell · Quarry Walk · Canesworde · Buttercup · Langdale Road · 30 · Queensbury School · Hilton Avenue · Kirkstone · Tarnside · Ullswater Rd · Bowland · Carmel Drive

Hurlock Cl · Ulverston Rd

1 grid square represents 500 metres

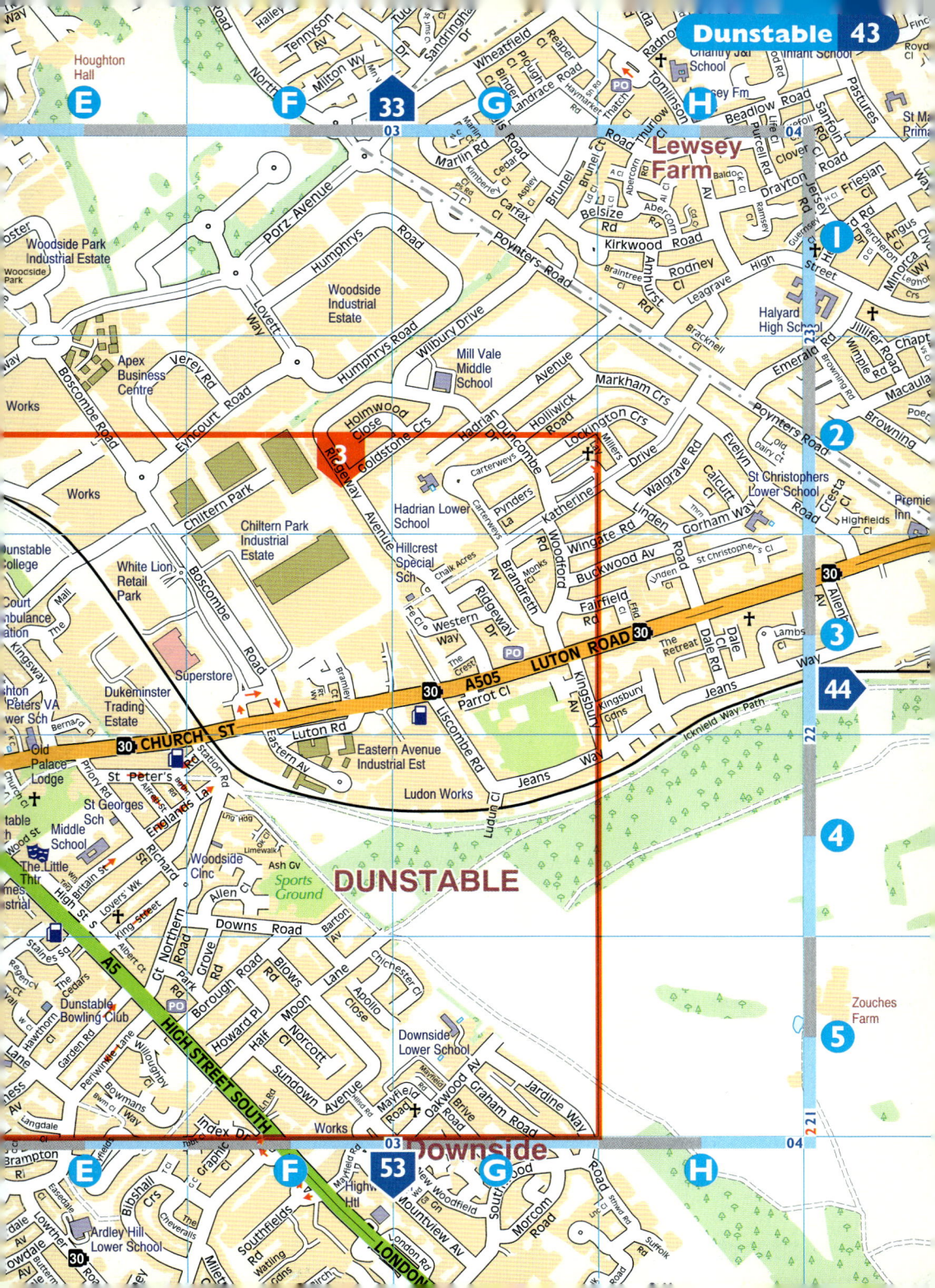

Lewsey Farm

DUNSTABLE

Downside

Houghton Hall

Woodside Park Industrial Estate

Woodside Park

Apex Business Centre

Woodside Industrial Estate

Chiltern Park

Chiltern Park Industrial Estate

White Lion Retail Park

Dukeminster Trading Estate

Works

Works

Dunstable College

Court Ambulance Station

Kingsway

Ashton Peters VA Lower Sch

Old Palace Lodge

St Peter's

St Georges Sch

Dunstable Middle School

The Little Theatre

Dunstable Bowling Club

The Cedars

Hadrian Lower School

Hillcrest Special Sch

Mill Vale Middle School

Holmwood Close

Goldstone Cres

Chalk Acres

Superstore

Eastern Avenue Industrial Est

Ludon Works

Woodside Clinic

Sports Ground

Ash Gv

Downside Lower School

Halyard High School

St Christophers Lower School

St Christopher's Cl

Premier Inn

Highfields Cl

Zouches Farm

Ardley Hill Lower School

Charity J&I School

Infant School

St Mary's Primary

Roads / Streets

North Rd, Tennyson Av, Milton Wy, Halley Dr, Sandringham Dr, Tulip Dr

Wheatfield, Picot Rd, Reaper, Radnor, Tomlinson, Haymarket, Thatch, Beadlow Road, Purcell Rd, Life Cl, Clover Rd, Samfoin Rd, Jersey Rd, Pastures, Friesian Cl, Angus Cl, Minorca Cl, Cresta

Porz Avenue, Humphrys Road, Lovett Way, Verey Rd, Eyncourt Road, Boscombe Road

Marlin Rd, Cedar Cl, Carfax Cl, Brunel, Belsize Rd, Abercorn, Kirkwood Road, Braintree Cl, Amhurst Cl, Rodney Cl, Leagrave, Bracknell, Drayton Rd, Emerald Rd, Browning Rd, Wimple Cl, Macaulay, Jilliter Road, Chapt

Wilbury Drive, Hadrian, Duncombe Cl, Holliwick Road, Avenue, Markham Crs, Lockington Crs, Walgrave Rd, Evelyn Cl, Poynters Road, Browning

Ridgeway Avenue, Carterways, Pynders La, Katherine Cl, Miller's, Drive, Linden Rd, Calcutt, Gorham Way, Dairy Cl, Allen Way

Western Way, Ridgeway Dr, Brandreth, The Crest, Monks, Woodford, Wingate Rd, Buckwood Av, Unden, Fairfield Rd, The Retreat, Dale Cl, Dale Rd, Lambs, Jeans

CHURCH ST A505 **LUTON ROAD** A5

Parrot Cl, Liscombe Rd, Kingsbury, Kingsbury Gdns, Jeans Way, Ickneild Way Path

Station Rd, Eastern Av, Luton Rd, Priory Rd, Bernard, Alfred St, Englands La, High St S, King Street, Lovers Wk, Limewalk, Richard Rd, Allen Cl, Ling Hdg, Great Britain St

Northern Rd, Park Rd, Grove Rd, Borough Road, Downs Road, Blows Rd, Apollo Close, Barton Lane, Chichester Cl, Albert Ct, Regency Cl, Hawthorn, Garden Rd, Periwinkle Lane

HIGH STREET SOUTH A5

Howard Pl, Norcott Rd, Moon Cl, Half, Sundown Avenue, Index Cl, Willoughby, Bowmans Way, Bwm Cl, The Ridings

Mayfield Rd, Oakwood Av, Oakwood Drive, Graham Road, Jardine Way, Morcom Road, Southfields Rd, Watling, Highfield, Mountview Av, Woodfield, New Woodfield Gn, South

Bibshall Crs, Cheverells, Millfield, Lowther Rd, Owdale, Langdale Av, Suffolk

LONDON

33 E F G H I 2 3 44 4 5 53 E F G H

Leagrave

LU4

34 05

A St Martin de Porres Primary School

B

C Lea J&I School

D

Southfield Infant School

Chantry J&I School

Lewsey Fm Clinic

Lewsey Farm

Beadlow Road
Roydon Cl
Ravenhill Way
Runham Cl
Anmer Gdns
Finch Cl
Saltfield
Bank Cl
Orchard
Pigotts
School
Complin

Leagrave Health Cen

Moorlands School

St vnt Gdns
Wraysbury
Paisley Cl
Ouseley Cl
Ely Way
Oakley
Platt
Surr
Addington
Angel
Rodeheath
Clingwd
Villi

Purcell Rd
Drayton Rd
Lite Cl
Santill
Clover Rd
Baldo Cl
Beadlow AV
Rodney Road
Leagrave
High
Street
Glenside
Jersey Cl
Friesian Cl
Hereford Rd
Percheron Rd
Angus Cl
Clydesdale Rd
Suffolk
Way
Leagrave High St
Seabrook
Hebden Cl
Denton Cl
Dalby
Loftus Cl
Holgate Drive
Ickneild Way
Challney High School for Boys & Community Coll
Stonegate Rd
Wellgate
Homedale Dr
Fieldgate

Halyard High School
Minorca Cl
Leghorn Crs
Jilifer Road
Wimple Rd
Chapter House Road
Cloisters Rd
Carmelite Rd
Lime Avenue
Morcambe Close
Lewsey Road
Challney High Sch for Girls
Sandgate
Simpson

Emerald Rd
Browning Rd
Macaulay
Cresta Rd
Poets Green
Petard Dr
Shelley Road
Byron Road
Calnwood Road
Faringdon Road
Abingdon Road
Dunstable Rd

Poynter's Road
St Christophers Lower School
Gorham Way
Browning Road
Wordsworth Road
Highfields Cl
Premier Inn
Hayhurst Rd
Kendale Rd
Bampton Road
Luton & Dunstable Hospital
Luton & Dunstable Education Centre
A&E
Derby Rd
Eldon
Stanton
Overstone Road
Atherstone Road
Thirles
Weath

2 St Christophers Lower School

Junction 11

Allenby Way
Dale Rd
Jeans
Ickneild Way P
Combs
SWINPOT ROAD
Cradock
Ferrars Cl
Charlwood Road
Byfield Cl
Hayhurst Rd
Staveley Rd
Bakewell Cl
Ripley Rd
Longfield Dr
Raleigh Gv
Ar Gr
Halfway Avenue
Bradley
Cosgrove Way

30

3

43

Kiln Way
Works
Chaul End Road
A5065 HATTERS WAY
Toland Cl
M1
A506

4

Chaul End Road

5
Zouches Farm

Golf Course

Chaul End

A
B
54 05
C
D
Griffin Golf Club

22 1
5 04

I grid square represents 500 metres

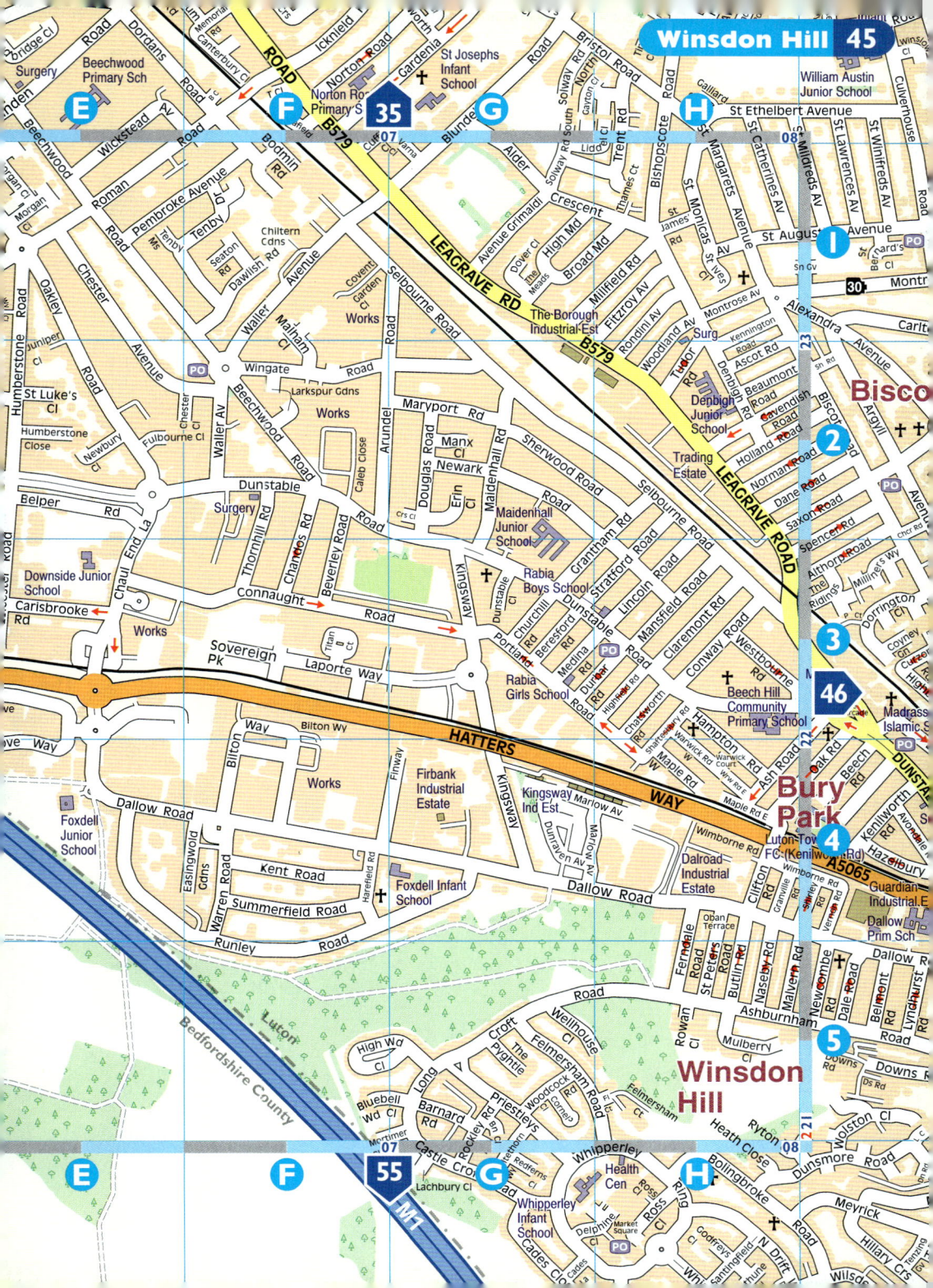

E
Beechwood Primary Sch
Surgery
bridge Cl
Dordans Road
Road
Canterbury Cl
Memorial
Icknield
ROAD
Norton Road
Norton Rd
St Josephs Infant School
Gardenia
Norton Road Primary S
F
35
Blunde
G
Bristol Road
Solway Rd North
Solway Rd South
Garton Cl
Lidg
Trent Rd
Bishopscote
Calliard
William Austin Junior School
H
St Ethelbert Avenue
Culverhouse

Wickstead
Beechwood Road
Roman Road
Pembroke Avenue
Bodmin Rd
Tenby Dr
Tenby
Seaton Rd
Dawlish
Chiltern Cdns
B579
Cliff
Varna
Alder
High Md
Avenue Grimaldi
Crescent
Dover Cl
The Meads
Broad Md
Millfield Rd
Fitzroy Av
Rondini Av
St James Ct
St Monicas Av
Montrose Av
St Ives
St Augus
St Catherines Av
St Margarets Avenue
St Lawrences Av
St Winifreds Av
Mildreds Av
Avenue
PO
I
Montr
30

LEAGRAVE RD
Covent Garden Works
Selbourne Road
Maham Road
Avenue
Waller Av
Morgan
Oakley Road
Chester Road
Humberstone Road
Juniper
St Luke's Cl
Humberstone Close
Newbury
Fulbourne Cl
PO
Wingate Road
Larkspur Gdns
Works
Maryport Rd
Manx Cl
Newark
Douglas Road
Erin Cl
Maidenhall Rd
Sherwood Road
B579
The Borough Industrial Est
Woodland Av
Tudor
Denbigh Road
Beaumont
Ascot Rd
Kennington
Alexandra Avenue
Carlt
Denbigh Junior School
Cavendish Road
Holland Road
Norman Road
Beresford
Trading Estate
Dane Road
Saxon Road
Spencer Rd
Althorp Road
The Ridings
Millisents Rd
Dorrington
LEAGRAVE ROAD
Bisco
Argyll
PO
2
Biscot Road
Aven
Coyney
Cutfer

Belper Rd
Chaul End La
Surgery
Dunstable Road
Thornhill Rd
Charlos Rd
Beverley Road
Arundel
Caleb Close
Crs Cl
Kingsway
Rabia Boys School
Churchill Rd
Portland
Dunstable
Grantham Rd
Stratford Rd
Lincoln Road
Mansfield Road
Claremont Rd
Conway Road
Westbourne Road
Downside Junior School
Carisbrooke Rd
Works
Connaught Road
Titan Ct
Laporte Way
Medina Rd
Rabia Girls School
Durban
Highfield Rd
Chatsworth
PO
Beech Hill Community Primary School
Hampton Road
Sharfenden Rd
Warwick Rd
Warwick Court
Ash Road
Oak Rd
3
46
Madrass Islamic S
The Ridings
P
PO
DUNSTA

Sovereign Pk
Bilton Wy
HATTERS WAY
Maple Rd
Kingsway
Wimborne Road
Oban Terrace
Bury Park
Luton Town FC (Kenilworth Rd)
4
A5065
Beech Rd
Kenilworth Road
Avondale Rd
Hazelbury
Guardian Industrial E

Firbank Industrial Estate
Kingsway Ind Est
Marlow Av
Dunraven Av E
Dalroad Industrial Estate
Clifton Rd
Granville
Henley Rd
Selbey Rd
Wimborne Road
Dallow Prim Sch

Foxdell Junior School
Dallow Road
Easingwold Gdns
Kent Road
Harefield Rd
Warren Rd
Foxdell Infant School
Dallow Road
Summerfield Road
Runley Road
Rowan Road
Ferndale Rd
St Peters Rd
Butlin Rd
Naseby Rd
Malvern Rd
Ashburnham Road
Newcombe Rd
Dale Road
Belmont Rd
Lyndhurst Rd
Dallow Road
5
Downs Ds Rd
Downs

Bedfordshire County
Luton
M1
Wellhouse Road
Croft
The Pyghtle
Felmersham Road
Mulberry Rd
Winsdon Hill
Heath Close
Ryton
Wolston Cl
Dunsmore Road
Meyrick
High Wd Cl
Long
Bluebell Wd Cl
Barnard Rd
Rockley Rd
Priestleys
Woodcock Rd
Camel
Redferns
Lothair
Delphine
Whipperley Ring
Bolingbroke
Ross
Ross
Ross
Hillary Cl
Wilsde

Mortimer
55
Castle Croft
Lachbury Cl
F
G
Whipperley Infant School
Cades Cl
Market Square
PO
Health Cen
H
Godfreys
Santingfield N
Drive
E

Biscot

Round Green

Bury Park

High Town

Winsdon Hill

Sto

Park Tow

A5228 STOCKINGSTONE ROAD

NEW BEDFORD ROAD

OLD BEDFORD ROAD

LEAGRAVE ROAD

DUNSTABLE RD B579

A5065

HOCKLEY WAY

TELFORD WAY

GUILDFORD STREET

CHURCH ST

ST MARY'S RD

PARK VIADUCT

CHAPEL VIADUCT

STUART ST

CHAPEL ST

William Austin Junior School

St Ethelbert Avenue

St Michael's Crs

Fountains Road

Cranleigh Gardens

Augustine Avenue

Montrose Avenue

Alexandra Avenue

Carlton

Denbigh Junior School

Denbigh High School

Alexandra Avenue

Marlborough Road

Lansdowne Road

Studley Road

Cromwell Rd

Brook Street

The Moor

Crawley Road

Stopsley High School

Luton Co-operative Sports Club

Wardown House (Luton Museum & Gallery)

Wardown Swimming & Leisure Centre

Wardown Park

Cricket Gnd

Pope's Meadow

People's Park

Richmond Hill Special School

Richmond Hill

Kingston Road

Ridgway Rd

Mountfield Rd

Woodbury Hill

St Matthews Infant Sch

Oxen Industrial

Abbeygate Business Cen

High Town Rec Centre

Luton Stn

Galaxy L Cen

Arndale Shop Cen

Town Hall

Police Stn

South Bedfordshire Magistrates Court

Crown Court

University of Bedfordshire

Mosque

Madrassa Islamic School

The Arcade

Guardian Industrial Estate

Dallow Prim Sch

Junior School

Infant Sch

Cemetery

Rec Ground

Bus Grg

36

45

56

I grid square represents 500 metres

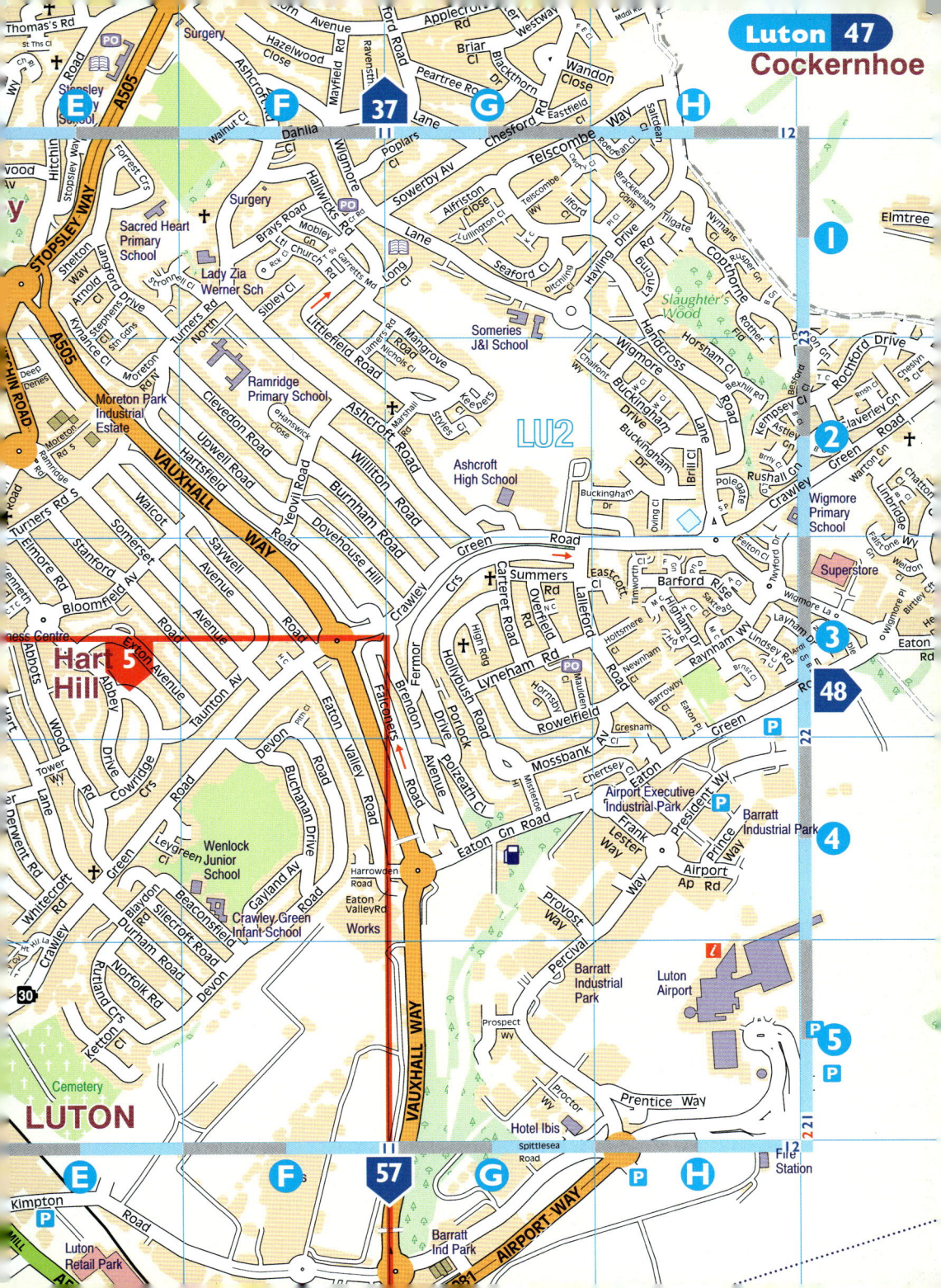

LU2

Hart Hill 5

LUTON

Cockernhoe

Schools & Places:
Sacred Heart Primary School
Lady Zia Werner Sch
Ramridge Primary School
Ashcroft High School
Someries J&I School
Wigmore Primary School
Wenlock Junior School
Crawley Green Infant School
Stopsley Primary School

Roads & Features:
A505
Stopsley Way
Hitchin Road
Vauxhall Way
Falconers Road
Eaton Valley Road
Airport Way
Luton Airport
Barratt Industrial Park
Airport Executive Industrial Park
Moreton Park Industrial Estate
Slaughter's Wood
Superstore
Hotel Ibis
Fire Station
Cemetery
Luton Retail Park

Prentice Way
Prince Way
President Wy
Frank Lester Way
Provost Way
Percival Road
Proctor
Prospect Wy
Spittlesea Road
Harrowden Road
Eaton Gn Road
Green Road
Crawley

Thomas's Rd
Hazelwood Close
Mayfield Rd
Ravensth
Applecroft Rd
Briar Cl
Blackthorn Cl
Peartree Rd
Wandon Close
Westway
Eastfield Rd
Chesford Rd
Telscombe Way
Saltdean
Dahlia Cl
Poplars Cl
Sowerby Av
Alfriston Close
Seaford Cl
Long Lane
Wigmore Rd
Halwicks Rd
Brays Road
Church Rd
Sibley Cl
Littlefield Road
Mangrove
Keepers
Elmtree
Rochford Drive
Flaverley Gn
Chattern
Green
Warton Rd
Eaton Rd

Turners Rd
North
Clevedon Road
Upwell Road
Hartsfield
Yeovil Road
Dovehouse Hill
Burnham Road
Williton Road
Ashcroft Road
Buckingham Drive
Horsham Cl
Handcross Rd
Codlinore
Haviland Dr

Elmore Rd
Stanford Av
Bloomfield Av
Somerset
Walcot
Saywell Road
Avenue
Taunton Av
Devon Road
Buchanan Drive
Abbey Drive
Cowridge Crs
Wood Green
Levgreen Cl
Gayland Av
Beaconsfield
Blaydon Road
Silecroft Road
Durham Road
Norfolk Rd
Rutland Crs
Ketton
Whitecroft Rd
Kimpton Road

Barford Rise
Lalleford Rd
Lyneham Rd
Rowelfield
Mossbank
Hollybush Rd
Portock
Polzeath Cl
Brendon Drive
Fermor Crs
Summers Rd
Overfield Rd
Carteret Road

Barratt Ind Park
Barratt Industrial Park

48

Cockernhoe

A B 38 C D

Green La
Mangrove Rd
Chalk Hill
Cockernhoe End Primary School
Stony Lane

Tea Green

Triggs Wy
Elmtree Av
Luton Road
Brickkiln Wood

Tilgate
Nymans
Colthorne
Rusper Gn
Rother Fld
Slaughter's Wood

Horsham Cl
Bexhill Rd
Cross Lane
Brill Cl
Polegate
Road

2

Litton Gn
Ripsey Cl
Bentley Gn
Bray Cl
Rushall Gn
Crawley
Green Road
Bedford
Rochford Drive
Claverley Gn
Watton Gn
Linbridge
Falstone Wy
Weldon
Chatton
Cheslyn Cl
High Cl
Rowington
Tameton
Rylands Heath
Hedley
Lennox Gn
Perrymead
Rosd
Road
Cutlers
Rise
Emmer Gn
Felbrigg Cl
Warminster
Ennismore
Malthouse Gn

Wigmore Primary School
Corbridge Dr
Colwell Rise
Lesbury Cl
Bsm Gn
Wh Cl
Hedley
Rl
Bowbrook
The Dell
Laxton Cl
Heaton Dell
Eaton Gn Rd
Superstore
Wigmore La
Birter Crt
Wigmore Pl

Barford Rise
Higham Dr
Raynham
Sawread
Twyford Cl
Felton Cl
Layham Rd
Keene
3
47
P
22

Wandon End

Hertfordshire County
Luton

President Wy
Prince Way
Barratt Industrial Park
Airport Ap Rd
P
4

Winch Farm

Dane Street

5
P
P

i
Luton Airport
Fire Station

Way

A B 58 C D

1 grid square represents 500 metres

Luton
Hertfordshire County

E F **39** G H

I

2

3

4

5

E F **59** G H

Stony Lane

Lilley

Church Road

King's Walden

Lilley Bottom

Church Road

Windmill Road

Windmill Road

Millway

Darley Road

Brownings Lane

The Heath

Heath Road

St Mary's Rise

Colemans Road

Darleyhall

Lower Road

Orchard Way

The Mdw

Oxford Rd

Chapel Road

†

Breachwood Green JMI School

Breachwood Green

Bailey's Farm

Lye Hill

Pasture Lane

Gro... Farm

Long Lane

Diamond End

Whiteway Bottom

Whit...

Park Farm

Works

To Dyers Rd

A

B

Greenway

40

The Orchards

C

D

4 96

21

20

Park Lane

97

The Comp

Comp Gate

I

Cantilupe Cl

PH

Wallace Dr

The Nurseries

Eaton Bray Lower School

Rose Ct

Northall Cl

Church La

High Street

School Lane

Saffron Rd

Gurney Ct

Eaton Bray

Northall Road

Church La

PO

The Meads

Perry Md

Eaton Pk

Medley Close

Knight's Cl

The Chqrs

Bower Lane

Moor End

2

Knolls Vw

The Sears

The Pepplatts

Eaton Bray Road

Cow

Yew Tree Cl

Moor End

Orchard Wy

Moor End

Mill End

Close

3

Beacon View

A4146

Broomstick Industrial Est

Summerleys

Good Intent

Orchard End

Jacksons Cl

PO

Waterside

M

Brook Street

Surgery

Wren Wk

Edlesborough

Cook's Meadow

St Mary Cl

Taskers Row

Tasker's Row

The Green

Dv Hs Cl

Slicket

4

2 19

LEIGHTON ROAD

Edlesborough School

High Street

Kings Mead

Pebblemoor

Church Croft

Chiltern Avenue

Brownlow Avenue

Swan

The Willows

Townside

5

4 96

97

A

B

C

A4146

LEIGHTON ROAD

D

30

Iwinghoe Way

St Leonard's Way

Totternhoe

Church Gn

Furlong Lane

Totternhoe Lower School

E   F   **41**   G   H

99   5 00

21

The Ride

Ellesmere Cl

Brightwell Av

Well

Church Road

Head Road

Church End

The Avenue

ICKNIELD WAY

B489

I

60

Dunstable Road

Doolittle Mill

Well Head

Manton Rd

Bottom Dr

Springfield Rd

B489

2

20

Bellows Mill

Harling Road

Bellows Mill Lane

TRING ROAD

3

52

Harling Road

Icknield Way Farm

4

219

5

LU6

ICKNIELD WAY

DAGNALL ROAD

Valance-end Farm

E   F   G   H

99   5 00

ICKNIELD WAY

B4506

TRING ROAD

WHIPSNADE ROAD

B489

ICKNIELD WAY

The Aven...
Beacon Ave
Coombe Dr
coomt...

Leighton Road
Royce Cl
Five Knolls

Pipers Croft

30
Meadway
Buttercup Cl
Canesworde

Road
...sborne Rd
Windermere Cl
First Aven...
Enterdale Av
Grasmere
Keswick
Appleb...
Langdale

42
Quarry...
Spoondell
Hurlock Cl

Queensbury School

Ulverston Rd
Mrln Cl
Bowland Crs
Hilton Avenue
Kirkstone Drive
Tanside
Staveley Road
Ulswater Rd
Cartmel Drive

Lark Rise Lower School

Road
30

A **B** **C** **D**

5 00
21
01
1

B4541

Icknield Way Path

Dunstable Downs Golf Club

Icknield Way Path

Golf Course

2

B489

Manton Rd

20

Dunstable Downs Country Park

Dunstable Downs

P

3

51

4

219

Icknield Way

Isle of Wight Lane

Isle of Wight Farm

LU6

Chute Farm

5

Works

5 00
01
A **B** 60 **C** **D**

S...prings

B4541

Tree
Cathedral (NT)

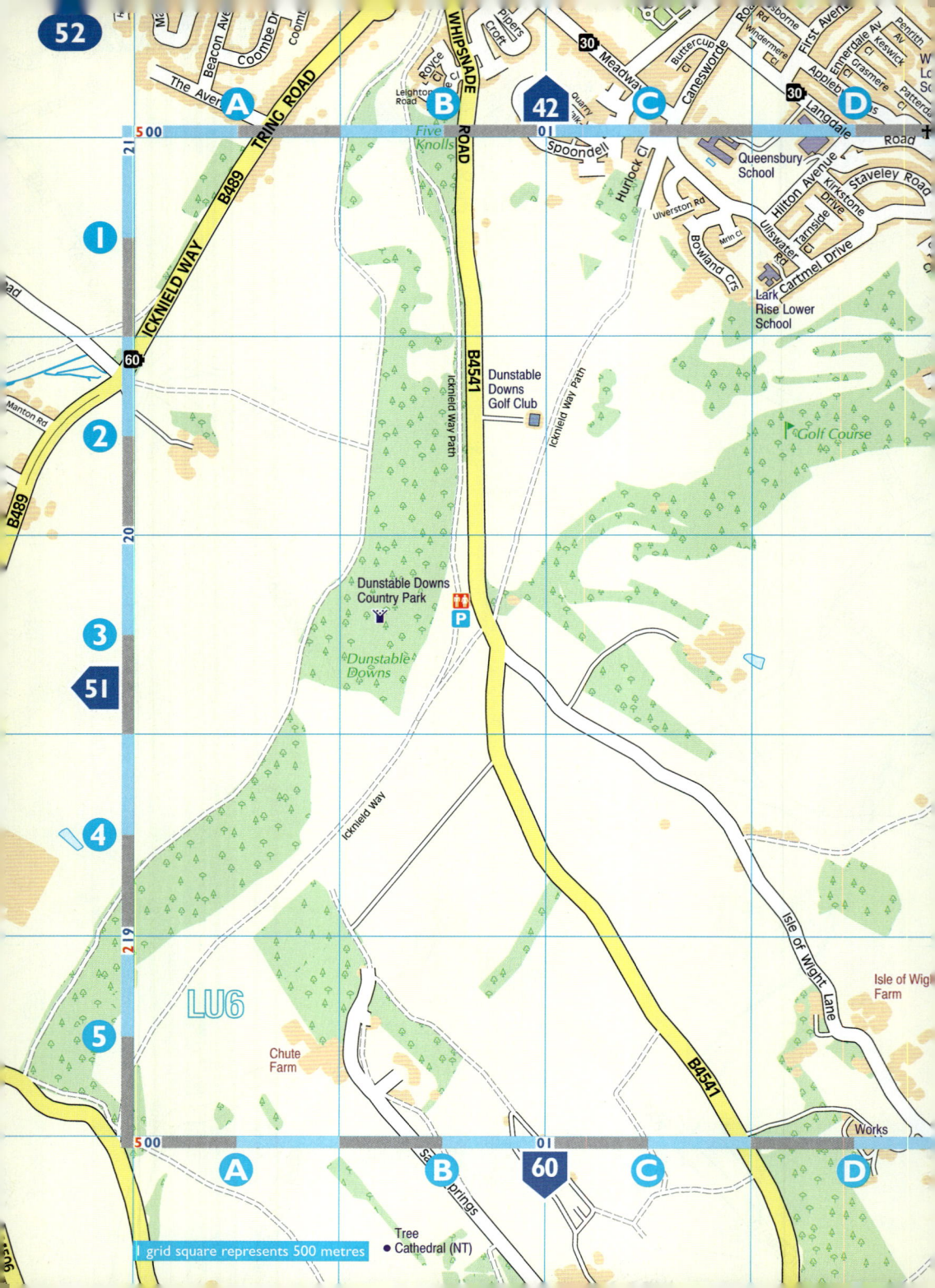

I grid square represents 500 metres

Dunstable
Bowling Club
Hawthorn
Garden Rd
Langdale
Lowther
Av
PO
Boro
Howard Pl
Moo
Norcott
Cl
Half
Sundown Avenue
Periwinkle Lane
Willoughby
Way
HIGH STREET SOUTH
Downside
Lower School
Mayfield
Oakwood
Road
Gr
Jardine Way
Road
Works
Index Dr

E   F   43   G   H
03   04
21

Downside

Hillyfields
Graphic Cl
Cl
Highwayman
Htl
Mountview Av
Mayfield Rd
New Woodfield
Southwood
Road
Morcom
Road
Norfolk Road
Strwd Rd
Suffolk
Rd

Brampton
Rl
Esscodale
Lowther
Av
Bibshall
Crs
The
Cheveralls
Ardley Hill
Lower School
Southfields
Rd
Watling
Gdns
London Rd
Side
Birch
LONDON ROAD
Lnc
Works
St Marys
Lower School
20

30
Road
Millestree
Abbey
Ms
Oldhill
Valence
End
Seamons Cl
Lockhart Cl
Burges Cl
Beech Cl
Streetfield
Middle
School
Manshead
School
Dunstable

Derwent Drive
Hill
Furzen
Close
Fox
Dells
Maundsey
Wayside
Lowther Road
Garrett
Churchill
Rd
Glenwood
School
A5
Turn
Farm
3

Mentmore
Knotts Cl
Brierley Cl
Ardley
Crescent

Beech
54

Beech Road
4

Church
End
219

Church
End
Hollick's
Lane

Hollick's
Lane

5

Kensw
House

Industrial
E   F   61   G   H
03   04

Common
Road
Spratts Lane
Nash
Farm
30
Corner
Farm

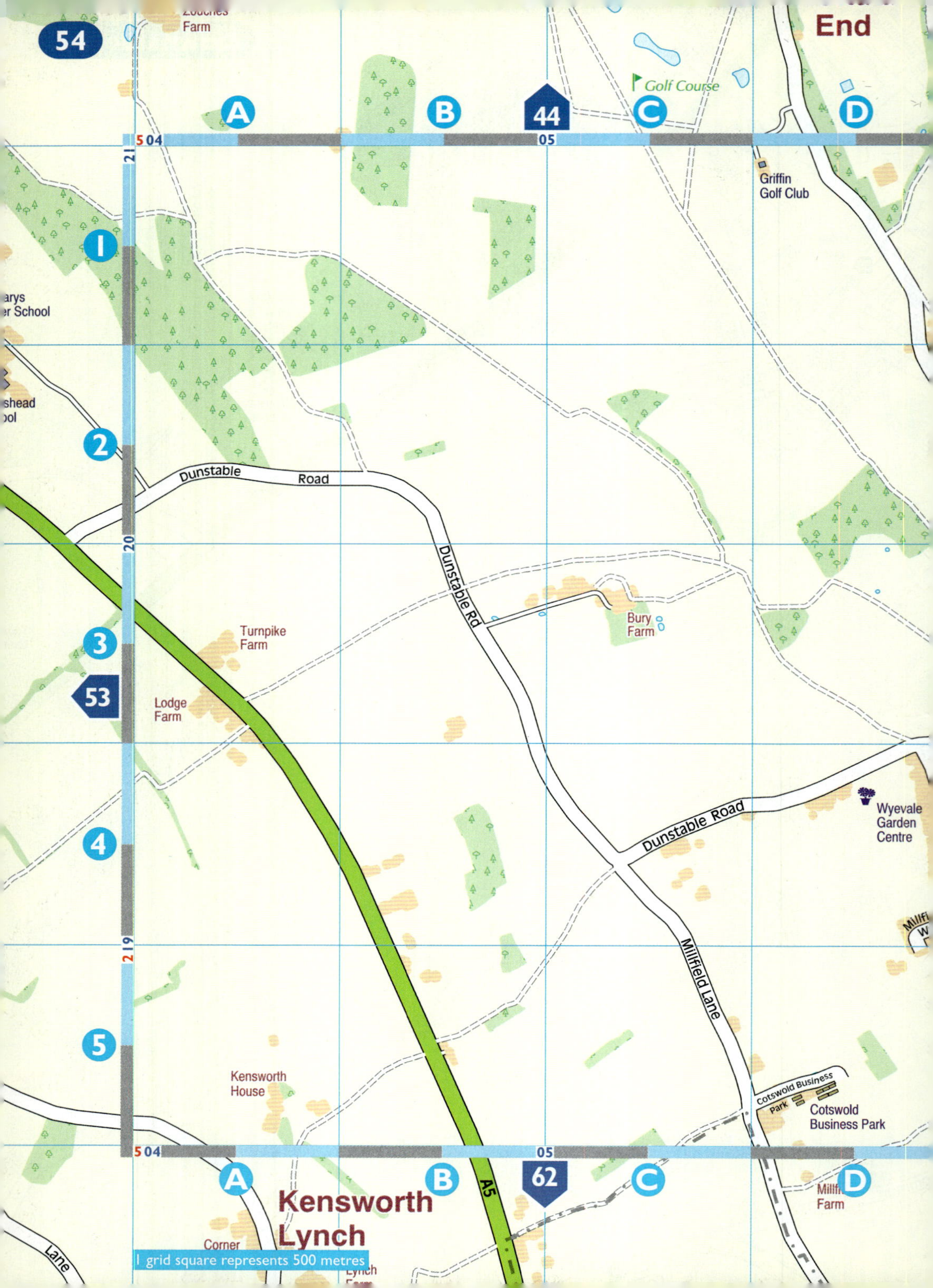

54

A   B   **44**   C   **End**   D

5 04   21   05

Zouches Farm

Golf Course

Griffin Golf Club

1

arys er School

shead ool

2

Dunstable   Road

20

Dunstable Rd

Bury Farm

3

Turnpike Farm

53

Lodge Farm

Dunstable Road

Wyevale Garden Centre

4

2 19

Millfield Lane

Millf W

5

Kensworth House

Cotswold Business Park

Cotswold Business Park

5 04   05

A   B   **62**   C   D

A5

Kensworth Lynch

Millf Farm

Lane

Corner

Lynch

Caddington

Winsdon Hill

Farley Hill

Woodside

Eley Green

Slip

E **F** **G** **H** **I**

45
55
56
63

Bedfordshire Col
Luton
M1

High Wd Cl
Long
Barnard Rd
Castle Croft Road
Rockley
Lachbury Cl

Croft
The Pyghtle
Wellhouse
Felmersham Road
Woodcock
Corner
Ct
Felmersham

Castleys
Whitethorn
Redferns

Whipperley Infant School
Whipperley Ring
Health Cen
Delphine
Market Square
PO
Cades Close
Cades

Bolingbroke

Ross
Godfreys
Santingfield N
N Drift
Bethune

Wulwards
Santingfield S
Richards
Drift
Friars
Wy
St John
Wy
The Gv
Masters
Rotheram Av
Friars Cl

St Margaret of Scotland Jun Sch
St Margaret of Scotland Inf Sch
Barnfield College

Roebuck
Olyard Court

Meyrick
Wilsden
Hilary Crs
Tenzing
Wy
The Cres
The Cres
Whipperley Way

Heath Close
Ryton Cl
Wolston Cl
Dunsmore Road

Farley Junior School
Whipperley Way
Farm
Gn
Homestead
Farley Hill
Odell Rd
Tingley Cl
Leyhill Dr
Farley Farm Rd

FARLEY HILL
B4540
Farleygreen

Inions Farm
Manor Farm

Luton Road

Caddington

Folly Lane
Chaul End Rd
Whipperfield
Meadow Way
H C
Hyde Road
Willowfield Lower School
Five Oaks Middle School
Heathfield Lower School
Orchard Cl
Delfield Gdns
PO
Surgery
Mossman Dr
Farm Cl
Crosslands
Manor Road
The Dell
Elm Avenue
The Crescent
Five Oaks
Culworth Cl
Adstone Rd
Ledwell
Fairgreen
Fairgreen Road
Enslow Cl
Edgecote Close
The Glen
Woodlands
Littlegreen Lane
Manor Road
Mardle Cl
Caddington Sports Club

Woodside Road

Woodside

Grove Park Road
Grove Road
Woodside Road

Pipers Lane
Manor Road
Cemetery
Elaine Gdns
Lower Farm

NEWLANDS ROAD
Luton RUFC
LU1
M1
2 19

CHURCH ROAD
St Andrew's
The Orchards
Prebendal Dr
Summer St
Front
Crawley
New
Rossway
PO
Slip End Lower School

Slip

60

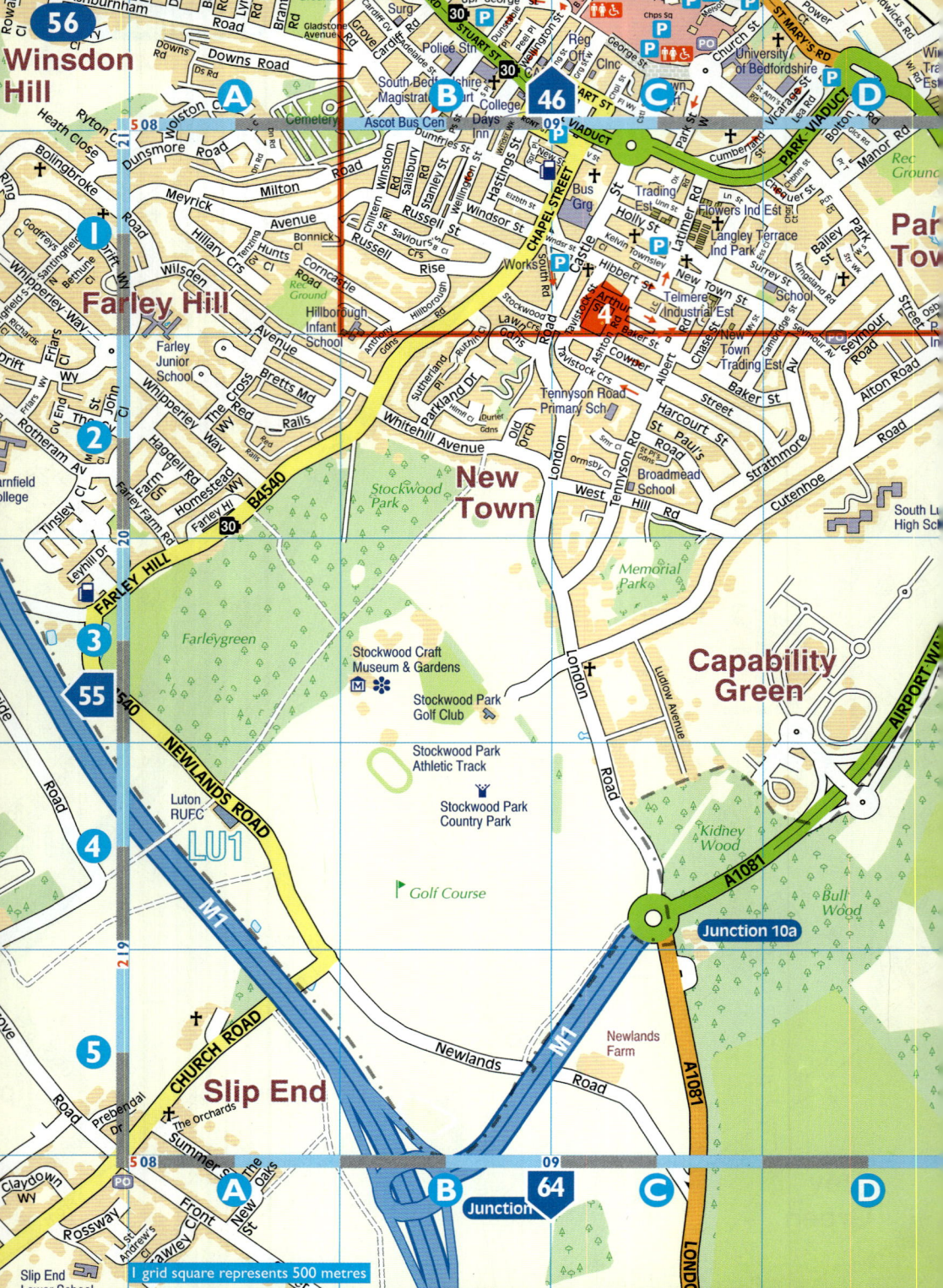

56 Winsdon Hill

Farley Hill

New Town

Capability Green

Slip End

University of Bedfordshire

Barnfield College

Farley Junior School

Hillborough Infant School

Farley Hill

Stockwood Park

Stockwood Craft Museum & Gardens

Stockwood Park Golf Club

Stockwood Park Athletic Track

Stockwood Park Country Park

Luton RUFC

Golf Course

Memorial Park

Kidney Wood

Bull Wood

Newlands Farm

Slip End Lower School

The Orchards

Tennyson Road Primary Sch

St Paul's

Broadmead School

South Luton High Sch

Langley Terrace Ind Park

Telmere Industrial Est

New Town Trading Est

Flowers Ind Est

Trading Grg

Bus Grg

South Beds Magistrates Court

Police Stn

Days Inn

Ascot Bus Cen

Chps Sq

Junction 10a

Junction

Roads: Downs Road, Dunsmore Road, Milton Avenue, Russell Rise, Whitehill Avenue, Newlands Road, Church Road, Farley Hill, B4540, London Road, Airport Way, A1081, M1, Park Viaduct, Chapel Street, Stuart St, Art St, St Mary's Rd, Pondwicks Rd

LU1

1 grid square represents 500 metres

Ketton Cr's
C1

Prospect Wy

Cemetery

LU☰ON

F

47

G

Proctor Wy

Prentice

H

Hotel Ibis

Spittlesea Road

Fire Station

Works

Kimpton Road

P

Luton Retail Park

A505

A505 GIPSY LANE

P 5

✈ Luton Airport Parkway Station

Barratt Ind Park

A1081 AIRPORT WAY

P

Vauxhall Road

Parkway Rd

P

I

Upper Lea Valley Walk

Somers

2

Someries Castle

1081 AIRPORT WAY

A1081

The Luton Dr

Lea Valley Walk

Bush Pasture

ower Kidney Vood

20

3

58

4

George Wood

Luton Drive

B653

Luton Hoo Park

The Luton

River Lea or Lee

LOWER HARPENDEN ROAD

2 19

5

Luton Hoo Hotel

Lea Valley Walk

E

F

65

G

H

The Warren Drive

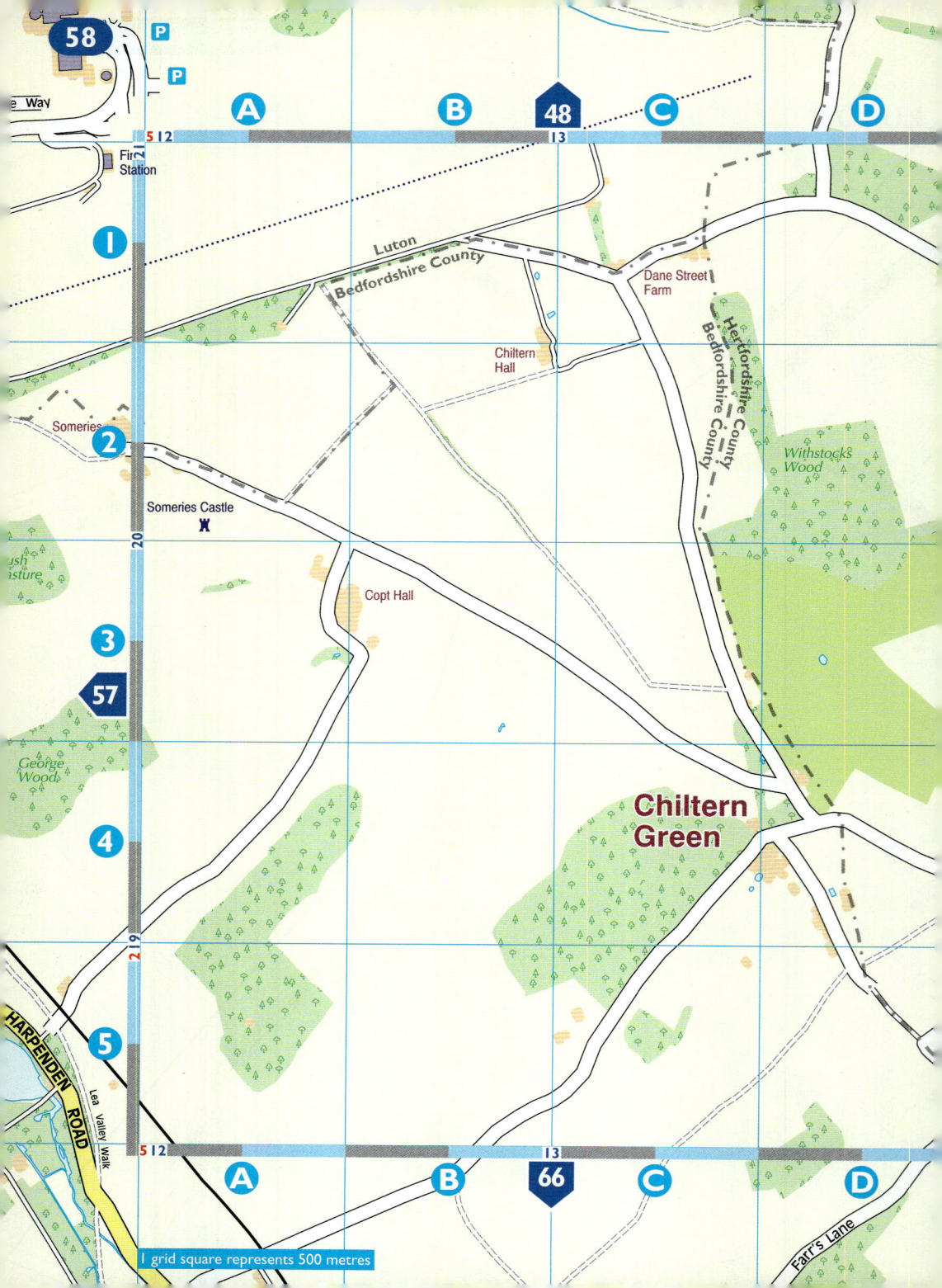

58

P

P

e Way

A

B

48

C

D

5 12

13

Fire Station

I

Luton
Bedfordshire County

Dane Street
Farm

Chiltern
Hall

Somenes

2

Hertfordshire County
Bedfordshire County

Withstocks
Wood

20

Someries Castle

ush
sture

Copt Hall

3

57

George
Wood

4

Chiltern
Green

2 19

5

HARPENDEN ROAD

Lea Valley Walk

5 12

13

A

B

66

C

D

Farr's Lane

I grid square represents 500 metres

E F **49** G H

15 16 21

Long Lane

Whiteway Bottom

Diamond End

Whitewaybottom

I

Wandon Green Farm

Lawrence End Rd

2

20

wrence End

Road

Rudwick Hall

3

Whitewaybottom

Barleybeans

Lawrence

End

Lane

4

Peters Green

The Green

Lane

2 19 Luton Road

Ansells End

5

Kimpton Road

E F **67** G H

15 16

Great Plummers Farm

Ramridge Farm

Plum

Skegs

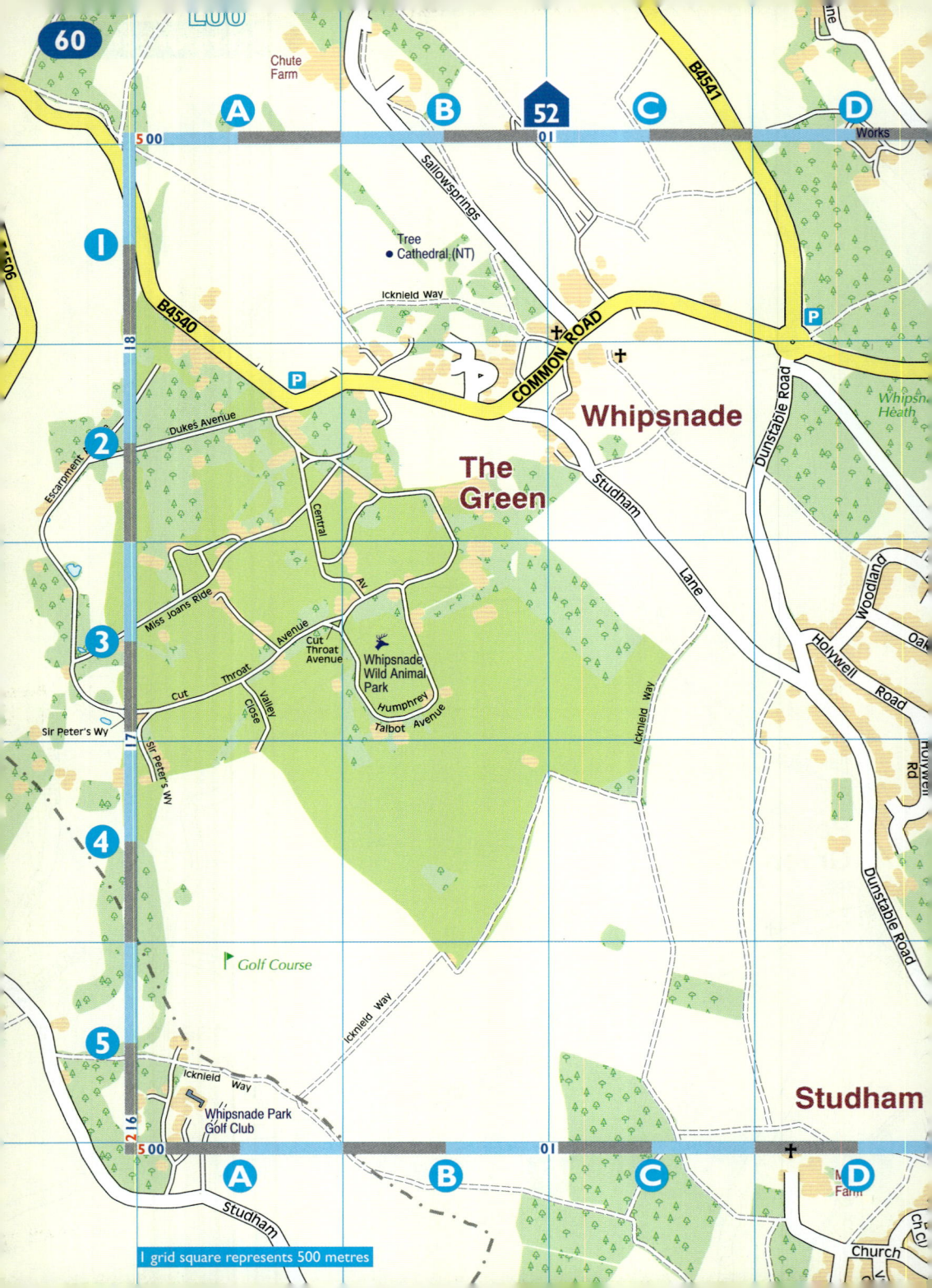

LUU

Chute Farm

A

B

52

C

B4541

D

Works

I

Sallowsprings

Tree
● Cathedral (NT)

5 00

01

B4540

Icknield Way

P

COMMON ROAD

✠

P

Whipsnade

Whipsn
Heath

Dukes Avenue

2

The
Green

Studham

Dunstable Road

Escarpment

Central

Av

Lane

Woodland

Oak

3

Miss Joans Ride

Avenue

Cut
Throat
Avenue

Whipsnade
Wild Animal
Park

Icknield Way

Holywell Road

Holywell
Rd

Cut

Throat

Valley

Close

Humphrey

Talbot Avenue

Sir Peter's Wy

Sir Peter's Wy

4

Golf Course

Dunstable Road

Icknield Way

5

Icknield Way

Studham

Whipsnade Park
Golf Club

2 16

5 00

01

✠

A

B

C

D

M
Farm

Studham

Church

I grid square represents 500 metres

E F 53 03 G H

Kensw
House

Industrial
Estate

Nash
Farm

Common Road

Hollick's Lane

Malms Cl

30 Common Road

Soratts Lane

Kensworth

Corner
Farm

I

B4540

Dove House La

Poplar Road

Maple Wy

WC

PO

Bakers La

Russell Cl

Ridgeway

Plewes Cl

Green La

Elmside

House Lane

Dove Lane

Buckwood Lane

COMMON ROAD

Wick Hill

B4540

LYN

The Chilterns

Kensworth
Lower
School

Hall Road

18

2

Clay

3

62 Bedfo
Hertfo

17

Holywell

Oldhill
Wood

Byslips Road

Dedmansey
Wood

Buckwo

4

Byslips Road

Hill
Farm

Byslips

Byslips

Buck
Stubs

5

216

South Wy

Wood

Kensworth Road

03 04

E F G H

Roe En

A B 54 C D

Kensworth House

Cotswold Business Park

Cotswold Business Park

5 04 05

Kensworth Lynch

A5

Millfield Farm

I

Corner Farm

Lynch Farm

Lane

18

Wick Hill

B4540 LYNCH HILL

ROAD

Road

Kensworth Lower School

Red Cow Farm

Hall

2

3

A5

Mark Cell

61

17

Bedfordshire County

Hertfordshire County

Buckwood Road

High St

Cemetery

View

4

Dedmansey Woods

Markyate Village School

Grange

Cavendish Rd

Cowper Road

Becks Cl

Buckwood Stubs

5

Parkfield

Corner Wood

Park Cl

The Coppins

Pickford

216

Cheverells Cl

5 04 05

A B C D

Roe End

Sebright School

Chever Green

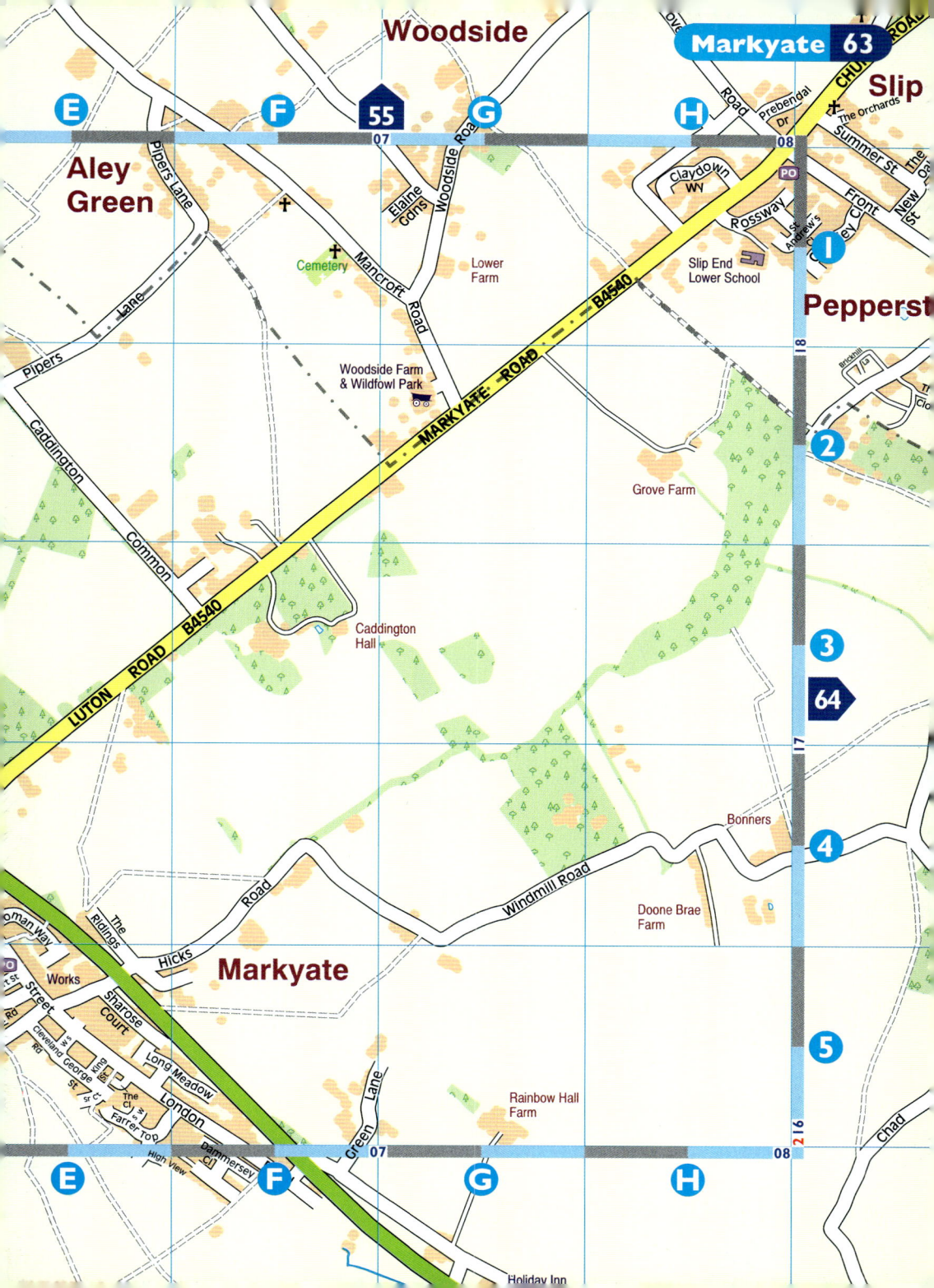

Woodside

Slip

E F 55 G H

07 08

Aley Green

Pipers Lane

Elaine Gdns

Woodside Road

Lower Farm

Claydown Wy

Prebendal Dr

The Orchards

Summer St

The Oak

PO

Front

New St

Rossway

St Andrew's

Cemetery

Mancroft Road

Slip End Lower School

I

Pepperst

Caddington Common

Pipers Lane

MARKYATE ROAD B4540

Woodside Farm & Wildfowl Park

Grove Farm

Brickhill

7/4

Cloi

2

18

Caddington Hall

LUTON ROAD B4540

3

64

17

Bonners

4

Road

The Ridings

Hicks

Windmill Road

Doone Brae Farm

D

Works

Roman Way

St St

Rd

Sharose Court

Cleveland George

Long Meadow

London

The Cl

Farrer

Markyate

Green Lane

Rainbow Hall Farm

5

2 16

Dammersey Cl

High View

Chad

E F G H

07 08

Holiday Inn

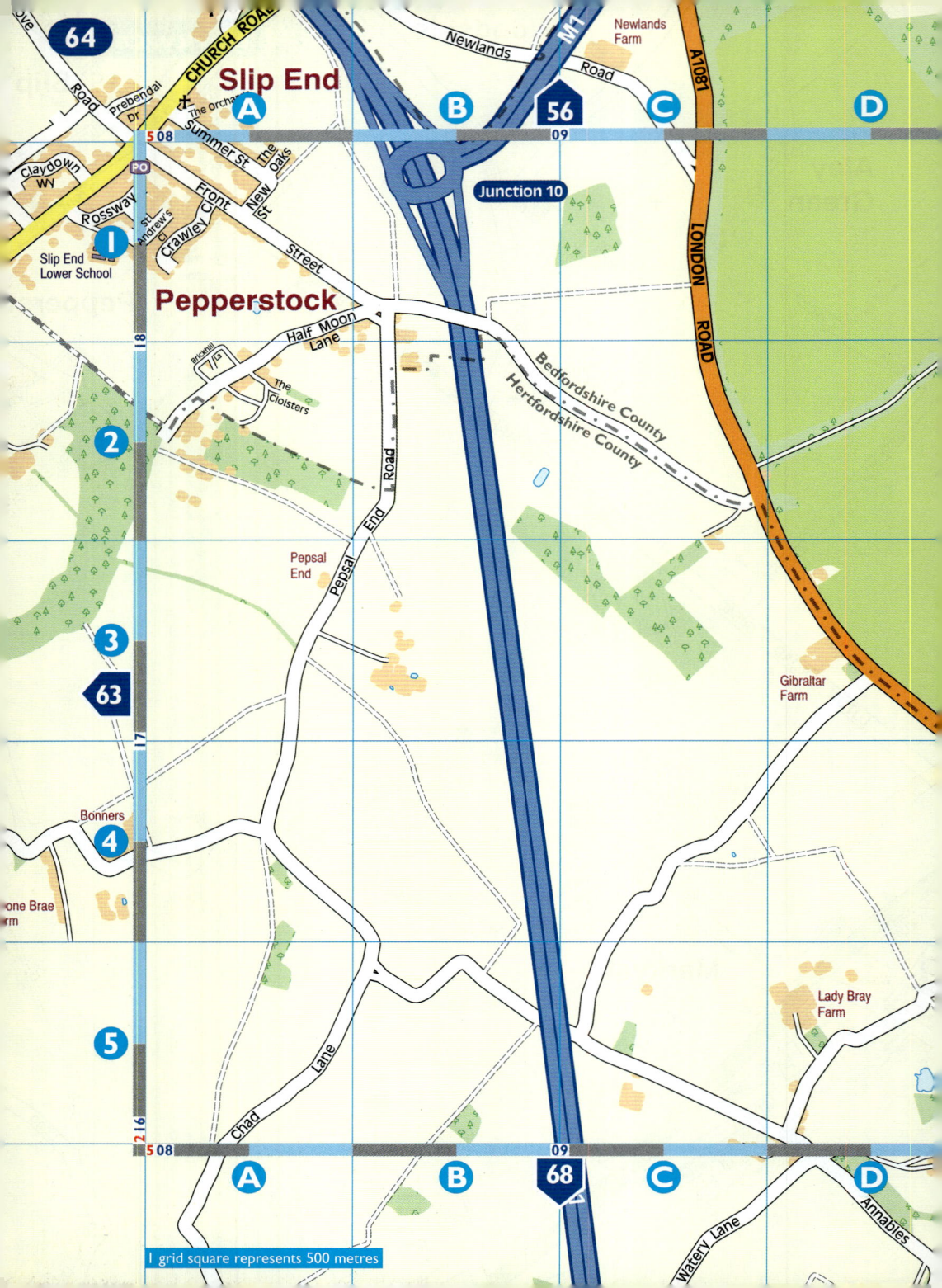

64

64

Slip End

CHURCH ROAD

Newlands

M1

Newlands Farm Road

A1081

LONDON ROAD

A

B

56

C

D

5 08

Summer St

Prebendal Dr

The Orchard

Claydown Wy

Rossway

PO

St Andrew's Cl

Front

New St

Crawley

The Oaks

Street

Junction 10

09

Slip End Lower School

1

Pepperstock

Half Moon Lane

Brickhill

the Cloisters

2

Bedfordshire County

Hertfordshire County

Pepsal End

Pepsal End Road

18

3

63

17

Gibraltar Farm

Bonners

4

one Brae rm

Lady Bray Farm

5

216

Chad Lane

5 08

A

B

68

09

C

Watery Lane

D

Annables

I grid square represents 500 metres

E

F

57

G

H

12

I

18

New Mill End

2

Lea Valley Walk

LOWE

HAMDEN ROAD

Luton Hoo Hotel

The

The Warren Drive

Birch Wood

Home Farm

3

66

17

West Hyde

Farm Road

Limetree

Avenue

Lady Bute's Lodge

4

LONDON ROAD

Kennel

Lane

Thrales End

Thrales

5

Kinsbourne Green

Common

Thrales End Lane

PO

Chamberlaines

Spring Road

E

F

69

G

The

Derwent Road

Kinsbourne Cl

Tintern Cl

Crosspath

Shphr Wy

The Close

The Pleasance

H

K Crs

Vale Cl

Prishrs

Cl

Farm Av

Moler

Luton R

Way

12

2 16

66

HARPENDEN ROAD

Lea Valley Walk

A   B   58   C   D

5 1 2   1 3

1

8

New Mill End

LOWER HARPENDEN ROAD

2

East Hyde

Southern Rise

Hambro Close

Farr's Lane

The Hyde

Hy
Fa

3

65

17

Lea Valley Walk

Great C
Farm

Westfield

B653

40

River Lea or Lee

4

40

Lea Valley Walk

End

Road

LOWER

Thrales

Bedfordshire County

Hertfordshire County

LUTON

5

Thrales End

Thrales End Lane

2 1 6

5 1 2   1 3

A   B   70   C   D

Cooters End Lane

The Kings School

Springfield

Crs

Moorland

Road

Riverford

Westfield

Drive

Westfield

Gilber
Ct

asance

K Crs

nshrs

Vale Cl

Farm Av

Molesw

The Lea
Primary
School

Hyde

Westfield

Way

idge Av

Bro Rd

Harpenden

1 grid square represents 500 metres

End

E F **59** G H

15

I

Skegsbury Lane

Kimpton Road

Great Plummers
Farm

Ramridge
Farm

Plummers Lane

18

Tallents
Farm

2

Hill
Farm

BOTTOM

**Porte
End**

Dane Farm

B652

KIMPTON

3

Holly

17

Lane

Blackr

4

Bower Heath

Lane

HEATH LANE

Ks Hth
Pk

Sauncey Wood

Turners
Hall Farm

5

BOWER

**Cold
Harbour**

Common Lane

216

Saun
Wo

15 **71** G H

16

E F

30 **ROAD**

Saxon
Dane
mars Rd

Northfield Rd

Smrs
Rd

Noke Shot

30

Whitings Cl

Hill

Mill

Icey

Mackerve

A B 64 C D

09

I

5 08
16

Lane

Ch.

M1

Annables

Watery Lane

Farm

Hill & Coles
Farm

Turner's Hall
Farm

ng Street

River Hall

**Friar's
Wash**

2

A5

River Ver

15 Hill

River

Watery Lane

Junction 9

Flamstead

3

Express By
Holiday Inn

Chequers Hill

Priory
Orch

High St

PO

Singlets Lane

Church Rd Cemetery

Chapel
Rd

Trowley Hl Rd

College

Cl

Pie Cnr

Pie
Garden

Herts County
Agricultural
Showground

A5183

DUNSTABLE ROAD

Vicarage
Gdns

Parson's Close

4

Flamstead
School

Delmerend
Farm

Delmerend

Norringtonend
Farm

Norrington End

Hill

Hite Trowley

Hill Road

Limins Pond

12 14

Lane

Redding
Lane

**Trowley
Bottom**

5

M1

St Agnell's
Farm

5 08
09

72

A B C D

Lybury Lane

I grid square represents 500 metres

Thrales End

Kinsbourne Green

E   F   **65**   G   H

The Common

Spring Road

Chamberlaines

Annables Farm

Kinsbourne Green Lane

Roundwood Lane

Faulkners End Farm

Delgarth

Derwent Road

Kinsbourne Cl

Tintern Cl

Crosspaths

Tuffnels Way

Creazfield

Crpndrs Cl

Tuffnels Way

Yeomans Av

Wood End School

Yrmn Av

The Close

The Pleasance

PO

Shphr Wy

Vale Cl

Farm Av

Way

Molescroft

Wood End Hl

Wood End Road

Ashley Gdns

Hasingden

Brackendale Grove

Roundwood Lane

Roundwood Lane

Falconers Field

Ridge Avenue

Luton Rd

Ridgewood Drive

Wells

Woodlands

Gra

High Rd

Mayfield

Ridgwd Gdn

Roundwood Lane

How Field

Roundwood

Medlows

Springf

I

2

Roundwood School

3

70 Roundwood Prim Sch

Townsend Lane

Townsend La

Clay
Lane

Hartwell Garden

4

5

Ro...sted Experiment

Redbourn Golf Club

Golf Course

Luton Lane

dow Vw

E   **A5183**   F   **73**   G   H

Du

Thrales End Lane

II 12 16

15

2 14

A   B   66   C   D   LUTON

16   5 12   13

Bedfordshire Co
Hertfordshire Co

The Kings School

Harpenden Hospital

Springfield Crs

Westfield Drive

Moorland Road

Rye Hl

The Lea Primary School

Westfield Cemetery

Hyde Vw

Gilber Ct

Beechk

Cooters End Lane

Ambrose

Luton Rd

Ridge Avenue

Ridgewood Drive

MayField

High Rd

Woodlands

Applewood

Roundwood Lane

How Field

Park Rise

Roundwood

Harpenden Rd

Park Mount

Hill

Bloomfield Road

Hillside Road

Asquith Court School

Lmb Gdns

Amors La

Bryant Ct

Hollybush

Clarence Rd

Wordsworth Rd

Byron Rd

Highfield Oval

Lane

Lindley Close

Westfield Av

Dell Cl

St James Rd

Clarendon Rd

Jameson Rd

Ox Fallows

Lea Rd

Masefield Rd

Sauncey Av

Townsend Rd

Tennyson Road

Carlton Road

St Georges Sch Technology College

Stewart Road

Harpenden Memorial Hosp

Surgery

Cornwall Rd

Breadcroft

Ellis

Wood End
Wood End Hl
Wood End Road
Way
Ashley Gdns
Haslingden
Falconers Field

2

Park Rise

Park

Medlows

Moreton

Moreton Av

Roundwood Gdns

Newmans Drive

Broadfields

St Hildas School

Aplins Cl

Harpenden Health Cen

Hitherfield Rd

Lodge Gdns

3

Roundwood Park School

Roundwood Prim Sch

69

Claygate Avenue

Aiders End La

Townsend Lane

Salisbury Lane

The Bourne

Kirkdale Road

Sun

Bowers Wy

Vaughan Rd

High Rd

Surgery

Surgery

Oaklands Coll

Milton

STATION

Barns Dene

Hartwell Gardens

Longcroft Av

Park Av North

Maple Road

Rosebery Av

Kirkwick Avenue

AL5 Primary School

St A Av

HIGH STREET

A1081

Leyton Green

PO

Harpenden Station

Copped Beeches

4

Townsend Lane

South

Orchard Av

Rothamsted

Nicholas

Avenue St

Leyton Rd

Amenbury

Town Hall

Southdown Road

5

Rothamsted Experimental Station

Park Avenue

HARPENDEN

Harpenden Swimming Pool

Harpenden Sports Centre

West Common

Bull Rd

Harpenden House Hotel

St Dominic RC Primar School

Southdown Road

Sir Joseph's Walk

Alysdar

2 14

5 12   13

A   B   74   C   D   A1081

W Common
Redcote La

Cold Harbour

E F 67 G H

15 16

I

Common Lane

Sauncey Wood

Saucey Wood

2

30 ROAD

Turners End

Saxon Cl

Dane Cl

Smrs Rd

St Mrs Cl

Reynards Cl

30

Riverside Estate

Northfield Road

Porters

Noke Shot

Noke Shot

Hill

Hill Cl

Lwr Luton Rd

Pickford Hill

Pickford Hill

Fulmore Cl

Whitings Cl

Sauncey Wood Prim School

Milford H

Finley Rd

Milford Hill

Mackerye End

Mallard Ms

Allied Business Centre

Southview Rd

Roundfield Av

Salisbury Rd

Holcroft Rd

Tallents Crs

Lwr Luton Rd

Lwr va Wk

Batford Road

Batford

Lea Valley

Valley Rd

Manor Road

Castle Ri

Marshalls Way

Lwr Luton Rd

2

3

PO

Wroxham Wy

Waveney Rd

Marquis La

Marquis Lane

Marquis Cl

Cherry Tree La

Leasey Dell

Cross Way

Barton

Hickling

West Way

Manland Avenue

Langdale Avenue

B652

ROAD

Carisbrooke Rd

Granby Av

Glemsford Dr

Weybourne

Crabtree Lane

Holly Walk

Tylers Cl

Altwood

Lea Valley Walk

Leasey Bridge

Dalkeith Rd

Lyndhurst Drive

Lyndhurst Cl

Crasmere Av

Crabtree Junior School

Courtfields

DW

Thornbury

Brampton

The Cleave

Eng

Wn Cl Fl Cl

Waldegrave Pk

Ashwell Pk

Piggotts Hill

Golf Course

Leasey Bri Lane

4

214

Overstone Rd

Chesterton Av

Aldwickbury Crs

High Beeches Prim Sch

Hilltop Wk

Aldwickbury Park Golf Club

Gilpin

Crabtree

Fairmead Av

Highfield Av

Azley Gdns

Lane

Aldwickbury School

Wheathampstead Road

Poynings Close

5

Barnfield Rd

Rowan Brnf Rw

Birch

Piggottshill

Highfield Av

Way

Sherwoods

Sherwoods Rise

Wheathampstead Rd

Greenway

Aldwick Rd

High Firs Crs

Green La

Green La Rd

Long Buftlers

Croftwell

The Grove

Southdown Industrial Estate

Churchfield

Crans Wy

The Grove Junior School

Dark Lane

The Grove Infant School

Pipers Av

Grove

Sibley Avenue

Meadway

Paddock Wood

Ashcroft

Pipers

The Grove

E F 75 G H

15 16

borough Pk

PO

Southdown

Rd

St Michaels Cl

King Cl

Longfield Road

Vallance Pl

W Cl

Road

A B 68 C M1 D

St Agnell's Farm

Lybury Lane

1

Nicholls Farm

13

2

Tassell Hall

Police Station

Row Cl

Nich

eenlane rm

3

12

Flamsteadbury Farm

Lane

4

AL3

Gaddesden Lane

Holtsmere End

5

Lane

End

Holtsmere End

Great Revel End Farm

211

Ramada Hotel

ROAD

Aubrey Lane

A B C D

Holtsmere

TEAD

Nicky Line

1 grid square represents 500 metres

Little Revel

E F **69** G H

12

A5183

Redbourn
Recreation
Centre

Luton

Dunstable

Road

Blackhorse La
Lynsey Cl
Pipers Cl
Peppard Cl

Linden Rd

Aysgarth
Road

Bettespol
Mdw

Crouch

Cooper's
Cutt

Hall

Lane

Lords Meadow

Snatchup

Tingeys
Close

Rickyard
Mdw

Wheatlock
Md

Heybridge Cl

Redfield Cl

Lane

Cavan Rd
Holts
Crouch
Hall
Cotts
Crecy Cotts

Redbourn

Scout
Farm

Harpenden

Applecree
Grove

Cumberland
Dr

Lane

Ver Rd

Flint
Copse

Surgery

Redbourn
Infant
School

Meadow

High St

Miller Cl

Hawkes Dr

The
Ruins

T Mews

Common

Lamb

Road

Crown

Bassett

Hrdng

Phdam

Waterend Ln

Redbourn
Industrial
Centre

Health
Cen

Fish
St

Fs St F

Monks

St Mary's

North

Common

Hempstead
Rd

Silk Mill House
Museum

Brooke
End

Silk Mill
Rd

The Park

Brooke
End

The
Cl

Redbourn

Hemel

Chequer

Church End

Hempstead Rd

B487

St Albans Road

A5183

Chequer
La

The
Elms

Ver-Colne Valley Walk

A5183

I

B487

2

Harpenden
RUFC

Golf

3

74 Hammonds
Farm

4

5

13

12

12

211

E F G H

Beaumont
Hall

Beaumont
Hall

Lane

Redbournbury
Mill

Beesonend La

Redbourn

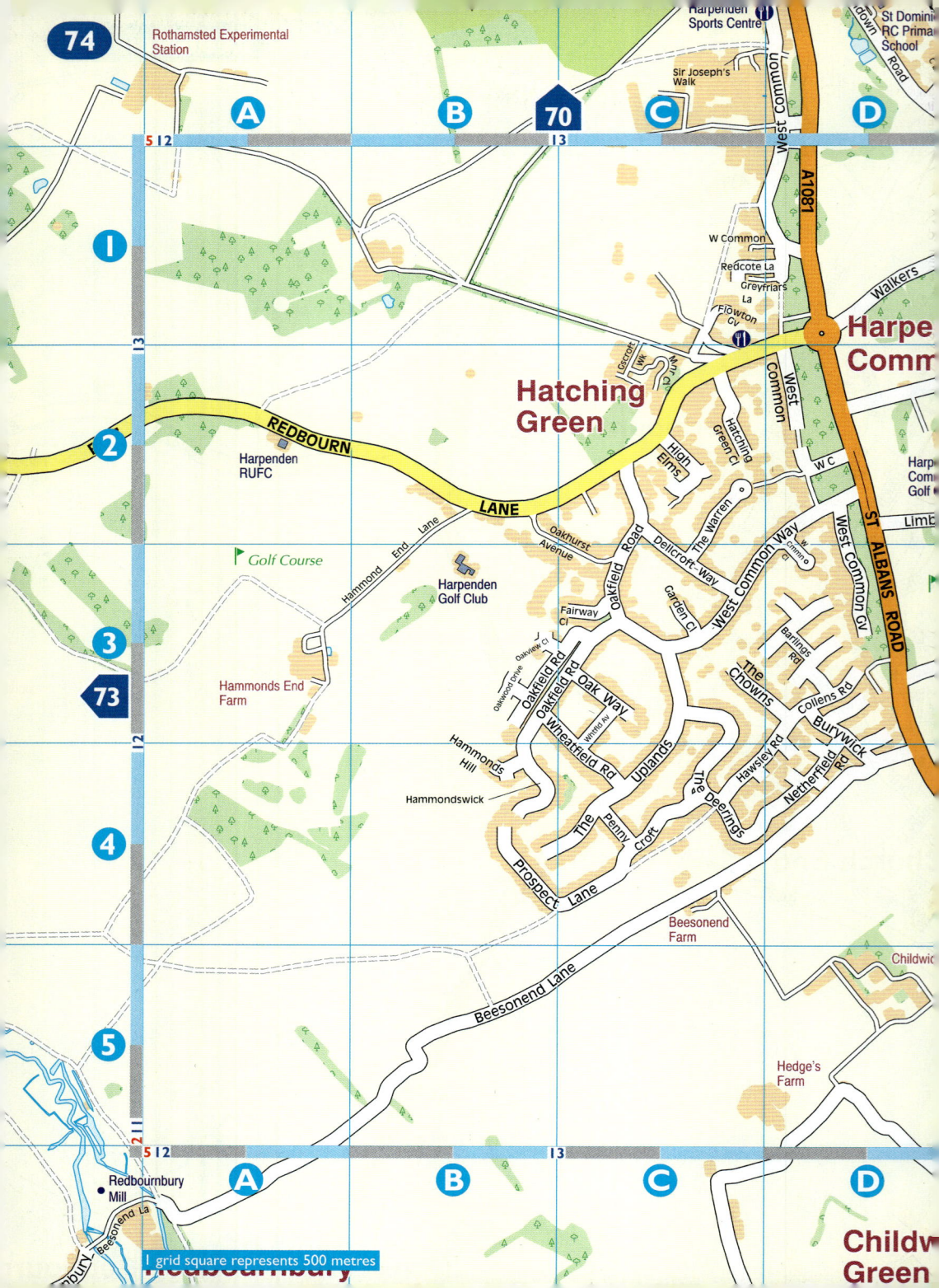

74

Rothamsted Experimental
Station

A   **B**   **70**   **C**   **D**

5 | 2 | 3

I

W Common

Redcote La
Greyfriars
La
Flowton
GV

St Dominic
RC Prima
School

Walkers

A1081

Harpe
Comm

2

REDBOURN

Harpenden
RUFC

LANE

Hatching
Green

High
Elms

Hatching
Green CI

The Warren

West
Common

West Common

W C

Harp
Com
Golf

Limb

ST ALBANS ROAD

Hammond End Lane

Golf Course

oakhurst
Avenue

Oakfield Road

Dellcroft Way

West Common Way

West Common Gv

3

Harpenden
Golf Club

Fairway

Oakfield Rd

Garden CI

comma

Barlings
Rd

73

Hammonds End
Farm

Oakview CI
Oakwood Drive

Oak Way

Oakfield Rd

Wheatfield Rd

limited Av

Uplands

Collens Rd

Hawsley Rd

Netherfield Rd

Burywick

The
Chowns

4

Hammonds
Hill

Hammondswick

The Penny Croft

The Deerings

Prospect Lane

Beesonend
Farm

Childwi

5

Beesonend Lane

Hedge's
Farm

Childwi

Redbournbury
Mill

Beesonend La

A   **B**   **C**   **D**

5 | 2 | 3

2 | |

5 | 2

Child
Green

I grid square represents 500 metres

Aldwickbury School

Topstreet
Way
Lane
Wheathampstead Rd
Wheathampstead Rd

Southdown Industrial Estate
Barnfield Rd
Rowan
Brnf Ct
Birch
Pigottshill
Churchfield
Sherwoods
Rise
High Firs
Gr
Aldwick Rd
Green La
Croftwell
Long Bu

E
F
71 15
G
H

The Grove Junior School
The Grove Infant School

I

Pipers

Marlborough Pk
Dark Lane
Pipers Av
Grove
Sibley Avenue
Leycroft Wy
Meadway
Paddock Wood
Ashcroft

The Grove

PO
Southdown Rd
St Michaels Cl
Grove
Field Cl
Hawthorn

Vallance Place
Oks Fld
Longfield Road
King Cft
Knowle Dr
Oakley Road
Barrons Rw

Pipers Lane

13

Coleswood Road
Broadstone Road
Tarrant
Magna
Parva
Eastcote Dr
Ranleigh Wk
Rise
Hdlg Ct
Cross Farm

Eastmoor Park
Cranbourne Dr
Fovant Cl
Burnsall
Acacia Wk
Nairn Cl
Aran
Welbeck Cl
Wensley Ct
Mons
C m Pl

Ayres

St Johns Rd
Eells
Eastmoor Pk
Little La
Grange Ct Rd
Beech Cl

West End Farm

2

End

Lane

Ferrers Lane

3

Ayres End

Cross Lane
Mud
Lane

12

Ayres End Lane

4

A1081

5

2 **11**

HARPENDEN ROAD

E **F** 15 **G** 16 **H**

Cheapside Farm

USING THE STREET INDEX

Street names are listed alphabetically. Each street name is followed by its postal town or area locality, the Postcode District, the page number, and the reference to the square in which the name is found.

Standard index entries are shown as follows:

Abbey Dr *LTNE* LU2 .... 5 G1

Street names and selected addresses not shown on the map due to scale restrictions are shown in the index with an asterisk:

Abbotswood Pde *LTNE* LU2 * 5 G1

GENERAL ABBREVIATIONS

ACC	ACCESS	CTYD	COURTYARD	HLS	HILLS	MWY	MOTORWAY
ALY	ALLEY	CUTT	CUTTINGS	HO	HOUSE	N	NORTH
AP	APPROACH	CV	COVE	HOL	HOLLOW	NE	NORTH EAST
AR	ARCADE	CYN	CANYON	HOSP	HOSPITAL	NW	NORTH WEST
ASS	ASSOCIATION	DEPT	DEPARTMENT	HRB	HARBOUR	O/P	OVERPASS
AV	AVENUE	DL	DALE	HTH	HEATH	OFF	OFFICE
BCH	BEACH	DM	DAM	HTS	HEIGHTS	ORCH	ORCHARD
BLDS	BUILDINGS	DR	DRIVE	HVN	HAVEN	OV	OVAL
BND	BEND	DRO	DROVE	HWY	HIGHWAY	PAL	PALACE
BNK	BANK	DRY	DRIVEWAY	IMP	IMPERIAL	PAS	PASSAGE
BR	BRIDGE	DWGS	DWELLINGS	IN	INLET	PAV	PAVILION
BRK	BROOK	E	EAST	IND EST	INDUSTRIAL ESTATE	PDE	PARADE
BTM	BOTTOM	EMB	EMBANKMENT	INF	INFIRMARY	PH	PUBLIC HOUSE
BUS	BUSINESS	EMBY	EMBASSY	INFO	INFORMATION	PK	PARK
BVD	BOULEVARD	ESP	ESPLANADE	INT	INTERCHANGE	PKWY	PARKWAY
BY	BYPASS	EST	ESTATE	IS	ISLAND	PL	PLACE
CATH	CATHEDRAL	EX	EXCHANGE	JCT	JUNCTION	PLN	PLAIN
CEM	CEMETERY	EXPY	EXPRESSWAY	JTY	JETTY	PLNS	PLAINS
CEN	CENTRE	EXT	EXTENSION	KG	KING	PLZ	PLAZA
CFT	CROFT	F/O	FLYOVER	KNL	KNOLL	POL	POLICE STATION
CH	CHURCH	FC	FOOTBALL CLUB	L	LAKE	PR	PRINCE
CHA	CHASE	FK	FORK	LDG	LODGE	PREC	PRECINCT
CHYD	CHURCHYARD	FLD	FIELD	LGT	LIGHT	PREP	PREPARATORY
CIR	CIRCLE	FLDS	FIELDS	LK	LOCK	PRIM	PRIMARY
CIRC	CIRCUS	FLS	FALLS	LKS	LAKES	PROM	PROMENADE
CL	CLOSE	FM	FARM	LNDG	LANDING	PRS	PRINCESS
CLFS	CLIFFS	FT	FORT	LTL	LITTLE	PRT	PORT
CMP	CAMP	FTS	FLATS	LWR	LOWER	PT	POINT
CNR	CORNER	FWY	FREEWAY	MAG	MAGISTRATE	PTH	PATH
CO	COUNTY	FY	FERRY	MAN	MANSIONS	PZ	PIAZZA
COLL	COLLEGE	GA	GATE	MD	MEAD	QD	QUADRANT
COM	COMMON	GAL	GALLERY	MDW	MEADOWS	QU	QUEEN
COMM	COMMISSION	GDN	GARDEN	MEM	MEMORIAL	QY	QUAY
CON	CONVENT	GDNS	GARDENS	MI	MILL	R	RIVER
COT	COTTAGE	GLD	GLADE	MKT	MARKET	RBT	ROUNDABOUT
COTS	COTTAGES	GLN	GLEN	MKTS	MARKETS	RD	ROAD
CP	CAPE	GN	GREEN	ML	MALL	RDG	RIDGE
CPS	COPSE	GND	GROUND	MNR	MANOR	REP	REPUBLIC
CR	CREEK	GRA	GRANGE	MS	MEWS	RES	RESERVOIR
CREM	CREMATORIUM	GRG	GARAGE	MSN	MISSION	RFC	RUGBY FOOTBALL CLUB
CRS	CRESCENT	GT	GREAT	MT	MOUNT	RI	RISE
CSWY	CAUSEWAY	GTWY	GATEWAY	MTN	MOUNTAIN	RP	RAMP
CT	COURT	GV	GROVE	MTS	MOUNTAINS	RW	ROW
CTRL	CENTRAL	HGR	HIGHER	MUS	MUSEUM	S	SOUTH
CTS	COURTS	HL	HILL			SCH	SCHOOL

SE	SOUTH EA...
SER	SERVICE AR...
SH	SHO...
SHOP	SHOPPI...
SKWY	SKYW...
SMT	SUMM...
SOC	SOCI...
SP	SP...
SPR	SPR...
SQ	SQUA...
ST	STR...
STN	STATI...
STR	STRE...
STRD	STRD...
SW	SOUTH WE...
TER	TRADI...
TER	TERRA...
THWY	THROUGHW...
TNL	TUNN...
TNL	TOLLW...
TK	TURNP...
TR	TRA...
TRL	TR...
TWR	TOW...
U/P	UNDERPA...
UNI	UNIVERS...
UPR	UPP...
V	VAL...
VA	VALL...
VIAD	VIADL...
VIL	VIL...
VIS	VIS...
VLG	VILLA...
VLS	VIL...
W	W...
WD	W...
WHF	WHA...
WKS	WO...
WKS	WE...
WY	WE...
YD	YA...
YHA	YOUTH HOS...

POSTCODE TOWNS AND AREA ABBREVIATIONS

Leopold Rd LBUZ LU7 ... 28 B2
Lesbury Cl LTNE LU2 ... 48 A3
Lester Ms LTNE LU2 * ... 4 C1
Leston Cl DUN/WHIP LU6 ... 53 F2
Letchworth Rd LTNN/LIM LU3 ... 35 F5
Levendale LTNW/LEA LU4 ... 34 C4
Lewsey Park Ct
LTNW/LEA LU4 * ... 34 A5
Lewsey Rd LTNW/LEA LU4 ... 44 B1
Leyburne Rd LTNN/LIM LU3 ... 35 H3
Leycroft Wy HARP AL5 ... 75 G1
Leygreen Cl LTNE LU2 ... 5 H2
Leyhill Dr LTN LU1 ... 55 H3
Leyton Gn HARP AL5 ... 70 C4
Leyton Rd HARP AL5 ... 70 C4
Library Rd LTN LU1 ... 4 C4
Liddel Cl LTNN/LIM LU3 ... 45 G1
Liddell Wy LBUZ LU7 ... 29 H4
Lidgate Cl LTNW/LEA LU4 ... 34 B3
Life Cl LTNW/LEA LU4 ... 33 H5
Lighthorne Ri LTNN/LIM LU3 ... 35 G2
Lilac Gv LTNN/LIM LU3 ... 22 C5
Lilac Wy HARP AL5 ... 75 F2
Lilley Bottom LTNE LU2 ... 38 C2
Lilley Bottom Rd
HTCHE/RSTV SG4 ... 49 G1
Lilleyhoo La HTCH/STOT SG5 ... 26 B4
Limbrick Rd HARP AL5 ... 74 D2
Limbury Rd LTNN/LIM LU3 ... 35 F5
Lime Av LTNW/LEA LU4 ... 44 B1
Lime Cl AMP/FLIT/BLC MK45 ... 9 E5
Lime Gv LBUZ LU7 ... 28 C1
Limetree Av LTN LU1 ... 65 E3
Lime Tree Cl LTNN/LIM LU3 ... 22 C5
Limewalk DUN/HR/TOD LU5 ... 3 G5
Linacres LTNW/LEA LU4 ... 34 D5
Linbridge Wy LTNE LU2 ... 48 A2
Lincoln Cl DUN/HR/TOD LU5 ... 53 G1
Lincoln Rd LTNW/LEA LU4 ... 45 H3
Lincoln Wy DUN/HR/TOD LU5 ... 12 A1
Lincombe Slade LBUZ LU7 ... 28 C1
Linden Cl DUN/HR/TOD LU5 ... 43 H3
Linden Ct DUN/HR/TOD LU5 ... 32 D5
HARP AL5 ... 70 D5
Linden Rd DUN/HR/TOD LU5 ... 43 H2
LTNW/LEA LU4 ... 35 E5
STALW/RED AL3 ... 73 E2
The Lindens DUN/HR/TOD LU5 ... 32 D5
Lindler Ct LBUZ LU7 ... 29 E3
Lindley Cl HARP AL5 ... 70 C1
Lindsey Rd LTNE LU2 ... 47 H3
Links Wy LTNE LU2 ... 36 A1
Linley Dell LTNE LU2 ... 47 H2
Linnet Cl LTNW/LEA LU4 ... 34 A5
Linney Head DUN/WHIP LU6 * ... 60 D4
Linslade Rd LBUZ LU7 ... 16 D2
Linwood Gv LBUZ LU7 ... 29 F3
Linwood Rd HARP AL5 ... 75 E1
Lippitts Hl LTNE LU2 ... 36 C4
Liscombe Rd DUN/HR/TOD LU5 ... 3 J3
Liston Cl LTNW/LEA LU4 ... 34 B4
Little Berries LTNN/LIM LU3 ... 35 E2
Little Church Rd LTNE LU2 ... 47 F1
Littlefield Rd LTNE LU2 ... 47 F1
Littlegreen La LTN LU1 ... 55 E5
Little La HARP AL5 ... 75 E2
LBUZ LU7 ... 18 C5
Little Meadow LTN LU1 * ... 55 H4
Little Wood Cft LTNN/LIM LU3 ... 35 E2
Liverpool Rd LTN LU1 ... 4 A4
Locarno Av LTNW/LEA LU4 ... 34 C3
Lochy Dr LBUZ LU7 ... 28 A2
Lockhart Cl DUN/WHIP LU6 ... 53 F1
Lockington Crs
DUN/HR/TOD LU5 ... 3 K1
Lodge Gdns HARP AL5 ... 70 C3
Loftus Cl LTNW/LEA LU4 ... 34 B5
Loire Ms HARP AL5 ... 75 E1
Lollard Cl LTNW/LEA LU4 ... 43 G1
Lomond Dr LBUZ LU7 ... 28 A2
London Rd DUN/WHIP LU6 ... 3 G7
STALW/RED AL3 ... 63 E5
Longbrooke DUN/HR/TOD LU5 ... 33 F5
Long Buftlers HARP AL5 ... 71 H5
Long Cl LTNE LU2 ... 47 G1
Longcroft Av HARP AL5 ... 70 B4
Longcroft Dr
AMP/FLIT/BLC MK45 ... 13 H1
Long Croft Rd LTN LU1 ... 45 G5
Long Cutt STALW/RED AL3 ... 73 E2
Longfield Dr LTNW/LEA LU4 ... 44 D3
Longfield Rd HARP AL5 ... 75 E1
Long Hedge DUN/HR/TOD LU5 ... 3 G4
Long La DUN/HR/TOD LU5 ... 10 C3
Long Md DUN/HR/TOD LU5 ... 32 D3
Long Meadow DUN/WHIP LU6 ... 2 B5
STALW/RED AL3 ... 63 E5
Lonsdale Cl LTNN/LIM LU3 ... 35 G4
Lords Cl LBUZ LU7 ... 30 C4
Lord's Hl DUN/HR/TOD LU5 ... 20 B5
Lords Md DUN/WHIP LU6 ... 50 C1
Lords Meadow STALW/RED AL3 ... 73 E3
Lords Ter DUN/WHIP LU6 * ... 50 C1
Loring Rd DUN/WHIP LU6 ... 42 B4
Lorrimer Cl LTNE LU2 ... 36 C3
Lothair Rd LTNE LU2 ... 37 E5
Lovent Dr LBUZ LU7 ... 29 F3
Lovers' Wk DUN/HR/TOD LU5 ... 3 F5
Lovett Wy DUN/HR/TOD LU5 ... 43 F1
Lower Harpenden Rd LTN LU1 ... 57 F2
Lower Luton Rd HARP AL5 ... 71 E1
Lower Rd HTCHE/RSTV SG4 ... 49 H3
Lowry Dr DUN/HR/TOD LU5 ... 33 F4
Lowther Rd DUN/WHIP LU6 ... 53 E1
Loyne Cl LBUZ LU7 ... 28 A2
Lucas Gdns LTNN/LIM LU3 ... 35 H1
Lucerne Wy LTNN/LIM LU3 ... 36 A5
Ludlow Av LTN LU1 ... 56 C3
Ludun Cl DUN/HR/TOD LU5 ... 3 J4
Lullington Cl LTNE LU2 ... 47 G1
The Luton Dr LTN LU1 ... 57 E2
Luton La STALW/RED AL3 ... 69 E5
Luton Rd AMP/FLIT/BLC MK45 ... 13 H2
DUN/HR/TOD LU5 ... 3 G4
DUN/HR/TOD LU5 ... 20 C1
HARP AL5 ... 70 A1
HTCH/STOT SG5 ... 26 C4
LTN LU1 ... 55 F3
LTNE LU2 ... 48 A1
LTNN/LIM LU3 ... 23 H1
LTNW/LEA LU4 ... 21 F4
STALW/RED AL3 ... 63 E3
Luton White Hl
HTCH/STOT SG5 ... 26 D4
LTNE LU2 ... 38 C1
Luxembourg Cl LTNN/LIM LU3 ... 34 D1
Lybury La STALW/RED AL3 ... 72 C1
Lye Hl HTCHE/RSTV SG4 ... 49 F5
Lygetun Dr LTNN/LIM LU3 ... 35 E3
Lynch Hl DUN/WHIP LU6 ... 62 A2
Lyndhurst Cl HARP AL5 ... 71 E3
Lyndhurst Dr HARP AL5 ... 71 E3
Lyndhurst Rd LTN LU1 ... 46 A5
Lynsey Cl STALW/RED AL3 ... 73 E1
Lynwood Av LTNE LU2 ... 47 E1
Lyra Gdns LBUZ LU7 ... 29 H1
Lywood Rd LBUZ LU7 ... 29 G3

M

Macaulay Rd LTNW/LEA LU4 ... 44 A2
Magna Cl HARP AL5 ... 75 F2
The Magpies LTNE LU2 ... 36 B3
Maidenbower Av
DUN/WHIP LU6 ... 42 B3
Maidenhall Rd LTNW/LEA LU4 ... 45 G2
Maldon Ct HARP AL5 ... 70 D3
Malham Cl LTNW/LEA LU4 ... 45 F1
Mallard Gdns LTNN/LIM LU3 ... 35 G4
Mallard Ms HARP AL5 ... 71 E2
The Mallow LTNN/LIM LU3 * ... 45 F1
The Mall DUN/HR/TOD LU5 ... 2 E3
Malms Cl DUN/WHIP LU6 ... 61 F1
Malthouse Gn LTNE LU2 ... 48 B3
The Maltings LBUZ LU7 ... 29 F3
Malvern Dr LBUZ LU7 ... 28 A1
Malvern Rd LTN LU1 ... 45 H5
Malzeard Rd LTNN/LIM LU3 ... 46 A3
Manchester Pl DUN/WHIP LU6 ... 2 C3
Manchester St LTN LU1 ... 4 B4
Mancroft Rd LTN LU1 ... 63 F1
Mander Cl DUN/HR/TOD LU5 ... 10 B5
Mangrove Rd LTNE LU2 ... 47 G1
Manland Av HARP AL5 ... 71 E3
Manland Wy HARP AL5 ... 71 E3
Manning Pl LTNE LU2 ... 48 A2
Mannock Wy LBUZ LU7 ... 29 H4
Manor Av LBUZ LU7 ... 18 C4
Manor Cl AMP/FLIT/BLC MK45 ... 7 G3
DUN/HR/TOD LU5 ... 11 H1
HARP AL5 ... 74 C2
Manor Farm Cl
AMP/FLIT/BLC MK45 ... 9 E5
LTNW/LEA LU4 ... 44 C1
Manor Gdns
AMP/FLIT/BLC MK45 ... 7 F2
Manor Pk DUN/HR/TOD LU5 ... 32 D5
Manor Park Dr
AMP/FLIT/BLC MK45 ... 7 F2
Manor Rd AMP/FLIT/BLC MK45 ... 14 B1
DUN/HR/TOD LU5 ... 10 B4
LTN LU1 ... 4 E6
LTN LU1 ... 55 E4
LTNN/LIM LU3 ... 22 B3
STALE/WH AL4 ... 71 H3
Mansdale Rd STALW/RED AL3 ... 72 D4
Mansfield Rd LTNW/LEA LU4 ... 45 H3
Manton Dr LTNE LU2 ... 36 B5
Manton Rd DUN/WHIP LU6 ... 51 H2
Manx Cl LTNW/LEA LU4 ... 45 G2
Maple Rd HARP AL5 ... 70 B4
Maple Rd East LTNW/LEA LU4 ... 45 H4
Maple Rd West LTNW/LEA LU4 ... 45 H4
Maple Wy DUN/HR/TOD LU5 ... 33 G3
DUN/WHIP LU6 ... 61 G2
Marbury Pl LTNN/LIM LU3 * ... 35 F5
Mardale Av DUN/WHIP LU6 ... 53 E1
Mardle Cl LTN LU1 ... 55 E5
Mardle Rd LBUZ LU7 ... 28 D3
Maree Cl LBUZ LU7 ... 28 A2
Margrett La
AMP/FLIT/BLC MK45 ... 8 D3
Marina Dr DUN/WHIP LU6 ... 42 A5
Market Ct LBUZ LU7 * ... 29 E2
Market Sq DUN/HR/TOD LU5 ... 10 C5
LBUZ LU7 ... 29 E2
LTN LU1 ... 55 H1
Markfield Cl LTNN/LIM LU3 ... 36 A3
Markham Crs
DUN/HR/TOD LU5 ... 43 G2
Markham Rd LTNN/LIM LU3 ... 36 A1
Markyate Rd STALW/RED AL3 ... 63 G2
Marlborough Pk HARP AL5 ... 75 E1
Marlborough Pl
DUN/HR/TOD LU5 ... 10 B5
Marlborough Rd
LTNN/LIM LU3 ... 46 A3
Marley Flds LBUZ LU7 ... 29 H3
Marlin Ct LTNW/LEA LU4 ... 33 G5
Marlin Rd LTNW/LEA LU4 ... 43 G1
Marlow Av LTN LU1 ... 45 G4
Marquis Cl HARP AL5 ... 71 F3
Marquis La HARP AL5 ... 71 F3
Marriott Rd LTNN/LIM LU3 ... 35 H3
Marshall Rd LTNE LU2 ... 47 G2
Marshalls Wy STALE/WH AL4 ... 71 H3
Marsh Rd LTNN/LIM LU3 ... 35 E4
Marsom Gv LTNN/LIM LU3 ... 35 H1
Marston Gdns LTNE LU2 ... 36 B5
The Martindales LTNE LU2 * ... 5 F4
The Martins Dr LBUZ LU7 ... 28 D1
Maryport Rd LTNW/LEA LU4 ... 45 E2
Masefield Ct HARP AL5 ... 70 D1
Masefield Rd HARP AL5 ... 70 D2
Masters Cl LTN LU1 ... 55 H2
Matlock Crs LTNW/LEA LU4 ... 44 C3
Matthew St DUN/WHIP LU6 ... 2 C4
Maulden Cl LTNE LU2 ... 47 G3
Maundsey Cl DUN/WHIP LU6 ... 53 E2
May Cl DUN/WHIP LU6 ... 50 C1
Mayer Wy DUN/HR/TOD LU5 ... 42 C1
Mayfield Cl HARP AL5 ... 70 A2
Mayfield Rd DUN/HR/TOD LU5 ... 3 H7
DUN/WHIP LU6 ... 53 F1
LTNE LU2 ... 37 F5
Mayne Av LTNW/LEA LU4 ... 34 C5
Maypole Yd DUN/WHIP LU6 * ... 2 D4
May St LTN LU1 ... 4 D7
Meadhook Dr
AMP/FLIT/BLC MK45 ... 8 D5
Meadow La DUN/HR/TOD LU5 ... 32 D4
Meadow Rd DUN/HR/TOD LU5 ... 20 A1
LTNN/LIM LU3 ... 35 H5
The Meadows
HTCHE/RSTV SG4 ... 49 G3
LBUZ LU7 ... 20 A5
The Meadow STALW/RED AL3 * ... 73 F3
Meadow Vw STALW/RED AL3 ... 69 E5
Meadow Wk HARP AL5 ... 71 E5
Meadow Wy HTCH/STOT SG5 ... 27 E3
LBUZ LU7 ... 29 H2
LTN LU1 ... 55 E3
Meads Cl DUN/HR/TOD LU5 ... 32 D4
The Meads DUN/WHIP LU6 ... 50 C2
LTNN/LIM LU3 ... 45 G1
Meadway DUN/WHIP LU6 ... 2 A7
HARP AL5 ... 75 G1
LBUZ LU7 ... 29 G1
Medina Rd LTNW/LEA LU4 ... 45 G3
Medley Cl DUN/WHIP LU6 ... 50 D2
Medlows HARP AL5 ... 70 A3
Mees Cl LTNN/LIM LU3 ... 23 F5
Melford Cl LTNE LU2 ... 47 H3
Melfort Dr LBUZ LU7 ... 28 A3
Melson St LTN LU1 ... 4 D4
Melton Wk DUN/HR/TOD LU5 ... 33 G3
Memorial Rd LTNN/LIM LU3 ... 35 F5
Mendip Wy LTNN/LIM LU3 ... 34 C1
Mentmore Crs DUN/WHIP LU6 ... 53 E2
Mentmore Gdns LBUZ LU7 ... 28 C4
Mentmore Rd LBUZ LU7 ... 28 C4
Mercury Wy LBUZ LU7 ... 29 H1
Merlins Ct LBUZ LU7 * ... 29 E2
Mersey Pl LTN LU1 ... 4 A4
The Mews HARP AL5 * ... 70 D4
Meyrick Av LTN LU1 ... 56 A1
Middle Gn LBUZ LU7 ... 29 G1
Middleton Rd LTNE LU2 ... 37 H5
Middleton Wy LBUZ LU7 ... 29 H4
Midhurst Gdns LTNN/LIM LU3 ... 36 A4
Midland Rd LTNE LU2 ... 4 C3
Midway LBUZ LU7 ... 29 G2
Milburn Cl LTNN/LIM LU3 ... 23 H5
Milebush LBUZ LU7 ... 28 A1
Miles Av LBUZ LU7 ... 29 F1
Miletree Ct LBUZ LU7 ... 29 F1
Miletree Crs DUN/WHIP LU6 ... 53 F1
Mile Tree Rd LBUZ LU7 ... 17 H3
Milford Hl HARP AL5 ... 71 F1
Millbank LBUZ LU7 ... 28 D1
Mill End Cl DUN/WHIP LU6 ... 50 D3
Miller Cl STALW/RED AL3 ... 73 F3
Millers Cl LBUZ LU7 ... 29 H2
Millers Lay DUN/HR/TOD LU5 ... 43 H2
Millers Wy DUN/HR/TOD LU5 ... 32 C5
Millfield La LTN LU1 ... 54 C4
Millfield Ms LTN LU1 * ... 54 D5
Millfield Rd LTNN/LIM LU3 ... 45 H1
Millfield Wy LTN LU1 ... 54 D4
Milligan Cl LTNW/LEA LU4 ... 34 D5
Milliners Wy LTNN/LIM LU3 ... 46 A3
Mill La AMP/FLIT/BLC MK45 ... 8 D5
Mill Rd DUN/HR/TOD LU5 ... 32 C5
LBUZ LU7 ... 29 E1
Millstream Wy LBUZ LU7 ... 28 D2
Mill St LTN LU1 ... 4 B3
Millway HTCHE/RSTV SG4 ... 49 F2
Mill Yd LTN LU1 * ... 4 D4
Milton Rd HARP AL5 ... 70 D4
LTN LU1 ... 56 A1
Milton Wy DUN/HR/TOD LU5 ... 33 F5
Milverton Gn LTNN/LIM LU3 ... 35 G2
Minorca Wy LTNW/LEA LU4 ... 44 A1
Miss Joans Ride BERK HP4 ... 60 A3
Mistletoe Hl LTNE LU2 ... 47 G4
Mixes Hill Rd LTNE LU2 ... 36 D5
The Moakes LTNN/LIM LU3 ... 35 E2
Moat La LTNN/LIM LU3 ... 35 H5
Mobley Gn LTNE LU2 ... 47 F1
Moira Cl LTNN/LIM LU3 ... 34 C3
Molescroft HARP AL5 ... 69 H1
Monks Cl DUN/HR/TOD LU5 ... 3 K2
STALW/RED AL3 ... 73 F3
Monmouth Cl
DUN/HR/TOD LU5 ... 10 A5
Monmouth Rd
DUN/HR/TOD LU5 ... 11 H1
Mons Cl HARP AL5 ... 75 F2
Montague Av LTNW/LEA LU4 ... 34 C3
Montgomery Cl LBUZ LU7 ... 17 F5
Monton Cl LTNN/LIM LU3 ... 35 F3
Montrose Av LTNN/LIM LU3 ... 45 H1
Moore Crs DUN/HR/TOD LU5 ... 33 E5
Moor End DUN/WHIP LU6 ... 50 D2
Moor End Cl DUN/WHIP LU6 ... 50 D3
Moor End La DUN/WHIP LU6 ... 50 D2
Moorhouse Pth LBUZ LU7 ... 29 H4
Moorhouse Wy LBUZ LU7 ... 29 H4
Moorland Gdns LTNE LU2 ... 4 B2
Moorland Rd HARP AL5 ... 70 D1
Moor St LTN LU1 ... 46 A4
Morar Cl LBUZ LU7 ... 28 A2
Morcambe Cl LTNW/LEA LU4 ... 44 B1
Morcom Rd DUN/HR/TOD LU5 ... 53 G1
Moreton Av HARP AL5 ... 70 B3
Moreton End Cl HARP AL5 ... 70 B3
Moreton End La HARP AL5 ... 70 B3
Moreton Pl HARP AL5 ... 70 B2
Moreton Rd North LTNE LU2 ... 47 E2
Moreton Rd South LTNE LU2 ... 47 E2
Morgan Cl LTNW/LEA LU4 ... 45 E1
Morland Cl DUN/WHIP LU6 ... 52 C1
Morrell Cl LTNN/LIM LU3 ... 35 G2
Morris Cl LTNN/LIM LU3 ... 35 E1
Mortimer Cl LTN LU1 ... 55 F1
Mossbank Av LTNE LU2 ... 47 G4
Mossdale Ct LTNW/LEA LU4 * ... 34 C4
Mossman Dr LTN LU1 ... 55 E3
Mostyn Rd LTNN/LIM LU3 ... 35 E5
Moulton Ri LTNE LU2 ... 4 E3
Mountbatten Gdns LBUZ LU7 ... 17 F5
Mountfield Rd LTNE LU2 ... 46 C2
Mount Grace Rd LTNE LU2 ... 37 G3
Mount Pleasant Av
DUN/HR/TOD LU5 ... 20 B2
Mount Pleasant Rd
LTNN/LIM LU3 ... 35 E4
The Mount LTNN/LIM LU3 ... 4 B2
Mountview Av
DUN/HR/TOD LU5 ... 53 G1
Mowbray Dr LBUZ LU7 ... 28 B2
Moxes Wd LTNN/LIM LU3 ... 35 E2
Mud La HARP AL5 ... 75 F3
Muirfield LTNE LU2 ... 36 C3
Mulberry Cl LTN LU1 ... 45 H5
Mulberry Pl STALW/RED AL3 * ... 73 F4
Mullion Cl LTNE LU2 ... 37 F5
Musca Ct LTNW/LEA LU4 * ... 45 F3
Mussons Pth LTNE LU2 ... 4 C2
Muswell Cl LTNN/LIM LU3 ... 35 H3
Mutford Cft LTNE LU2 ... 47 H3

N

Nairn Cl HARP AL5 ... 75 F2
Napier Rd LTN LU1 ... 4 A5
Nappsbury Rd LTNW/LEA LU4 ... 34 D4
Naseby Rd LTN LU1 ... 45 H5
Nash Cl DUN/HR/TOD LU5 ... 33 F4
Nayland Cl LTNE LU2 ... 48 A3
Nebular Ct LBUZ LU7 ... 29 G1
Needham Rd LTNW/LEA LU4 ... 34 B3
Nelson Rd LBUZ LU7 ... 17 F5
Neptune Gdns LBUZ LU7 ... 29 H1
Nethercott Cl LTNE LU2 ... 47 G3
Netherfield Rd HARP AL5 ... 74 D4
Nettle Cl LTNW/LEA LU4 ... 43 G1
Nettleton Cl LBUZ LU7 ... 29 G4
Neville Rd LTNN/LIM LU3 ... 35 G4
Nevis Cl LBUZ LU7 ... 28 A2
Newark Rd LTNW/LEA LU4 ... 45 G2
New Barn Farm La
DUN/HR/TOD LU5 ... 20 C5
New Bedford Rd LTN LU1 ... 4 B3
Newbold Rd LTNN/LIM LU3 ... 35 H2
Newbury Cl LTNW/LEA LU4 ... 45 E2
Newbury Rd
DUN/HR/TOD LU5 ... 33 G3
Newcombe Rd LTN LU1 ... 46 A5
New Fiddlers Hl HARP AL5 * ... 65 G5
Newlands Rd
AMP/FLIT/BLC MK45 ... 7 G3
LTN LU1 ... 56 B5
Newmans Dr HARP AL5 ... 70 B3
Newman Wy LBUZ LU7 ... 29 E2
Newnham Cl LTNE LU2 ... 47 H3
New Rd LBUZ LU7 ... 28 C2
New St LTN LU1 ... 4 B6
Newton Cl HARP AL5 ... 75 F2
Newtondale LTNW/LEA LU4 ... 34 C4
Newton Wy LBUZ LU7 ... 29 H3
New Town Rd LTN LU1 ... 4 D7
New Town St LTN LU1 ... 4 D7
New Woodfield Gn
DUN/HR/TOD LU5 ... 53 G1
Nicholas Wy DUN/WHIP LU6 * ... 2 D4
Nicholls Cl AMP/FLIT/BLC MK45 ... 8 D5
STALW/RED AL3 ... 72 D3
Nichols Cl LTNE LU2 ... 47 F2
Nicolson Dr LBUZ LU7 ... 29 H4
Nightingale Cl LTNE LU2 ... 37 G3
Nightingale Ct LTNN/LIM LU3 * ... 4 A2
Nine Lands LBUZ LU7 ... 18 D4
Ninnings Cots HARP AL5 * ... 70 C5
Ninth Av LTNN/LIM LU3 ... 34 D2
Noke Shot HARP AL5 ... 71 E1
Norcott Cl DUN/HR/TOD LU5 ... 3 G6
Norfolk Rd DUN/HR/TOD LU5 ... 53 G1
LTNE LU2 ... 5 H4
Norman Rd AMP/FLIT/BLC MK45 ... 9 E5
LTNN/LIM LU3 ... 45 H2
Norman Wy DUN/WHIP LU6 ... 42 A4
Norrington End
STALW/RED AL3 ... 68 C4
Northall Cl DUN/WHIP LU6 ... 50 B1
Northall Rd DUN/WHIP LU6 ... 50 B2
Northcliffe DUN/WHIP LU6 ... 50 C1
North Common Rd
STALW/RED AL3 ... 73 E4
Northcourt LBUZ LU7 ... 17 E5
North Drift Wy LTN LU1 ... 55 H1
Northfield Rd HARP AL5 ... 71 E1
Northfields DUN/HR/TOD LU5 ... 42 B1
North Star Dr LBUZ LU7 ... 29 G1
North Station Wy
DUN/WHIP LU6 ... 2 A1
North St LBUZ LU7 ... 29 E2
LTNE LU2 ... 4 C2
Northview Rd
DUN/HR/TOD LU5 ... 42 C2
LTNE LU2 ... 46 D2
Northwell Dr LTNN/LIM LU3 ... 35 F1
Norton Rd LTNN/LIM LU3 ... 35 F5
Nunnery La LTNN/LIM LU3 ... 35 H4
The Nurseries DUN/WHIP LU6 ... 50 C1
Nursery Cl DUN/WHIP LU6 ... 2 A4
Nursery Pde LTNN/LIM LU3 * ... 35 E4
Nursery Rd LTNN/LIM LU3 ... 35 F4
Nymans Cl LTNE LU2 ... 47 H1

O

Oak Bank Dr LBUZ LU7 ... 17 E3
Oak Cl AMP/FLIT/BLC MK45 ... 7 G2
DUN/HR/TOD LU5 ... 3 G5
DUN/HR/TOD LU5 ... 11 H2
Oakfield Rd HARP AL5 ... 74 B3
Oakhurst Av HARP AL5 ... 74 B2
Oakley Cl LTNW/LEA LU4 ... 34 D5
Oakley Gn LBUZ LU7 ... 29 F1
Oakley Rd HARP AL5 ... 75 F1
LTNW/LEA LU4 ... 34 D5
Oakridge Pk LBUZ LU7 ... 29 F4
Oak Rd LTNW/LEA LU4 ... 46 A4
The Oaks LBUZ LU7 * ... 17 E2
LTN LU1 ... 64 A1
Oakview Cl HARP AL5 ... 74 B3
Oakway DUN/WHIP LU6 ... 60 D3
Oak Wy HARP AL5 ... 74 C3
Oakwell Cl DUN/WHIP LU6 ... 42 B5
Oakwood Av DUN/HR/TOD LU5 ... 3 J7
Oakwood Dr HARP AL5 ... 7
LTNN/LIM LU3 ... 3
Oatfield Cl LTNW/LEA LU4 ... 3
Oatfield Gdns LBUZ LU7 ... 2
Oban Ter LTN LU1 ... 4
Offley Hl HTCH/STOT SG5 ... 2
The Old Bakery LTN LU1 * ... 5
Old Bedford Rd LTNE LU2 ...
Old Chapel Ms LBUZ LU7 * ... 2
Old Dairy Ct DUN/HR/TOD LU5 ... 4
Oldhill DUN/WHIP LU6 ... 5
Old Linslade Rd LBUZ LU7 ... 1
Old Orch LTN LU1 ... 5
Old Rectory Cl HARP AL5 ... 7
Old Rd AMP/FLIT/BLC MK45 ... 1
LBUZ LU7 ... 2
Old School Ct DUN/WHIP LU6 ... 5
LBUZ LU7 * ... 2
Old School Gdns
AMP/FLIT/BLC MK45 ...
Old Vicarage Gdns
STALW/RED AL3 ... 6
Olma Rd DUN/HR/TOD LU5 ... 4
Olyard Ct LTN LU1 ... 5
Olympic Cl LTNN/LIM LU3 ... 2
Omega Ct LBUZ LU7 ... 2
Onslow Rd LTNW/LEA LU4 ... 3
Orchard Av HARP AL5 ... 7
Orchard Cl AMP/FLIT/BLC MK45 ... 1
DUN/HR/TOD LU5 ... 1
DUN/HR/TOD LU5 ... 4
LTN LU1 ... 5
Orchard Dr LBUZ LU7 ... 2
Orchard End DUN/WHIP LU6 ... 5
The Orchards DUN/WHIP LU6 ... 5
LTN LU1 ... 5
Orchard Wy DUN/WHIP LU6 ... 5
HTCHE/RSTV SG4 ... 4
LBUZ LU7 ... 3
LTNW/LEA LU4 ... 3
Orchid Cl DUN/WHIP LU6 ... 4
LTNN/LIM LU3 ... 3
Oregon Wy LTNN/LIM LU3 ... 3
Orion Wy LBUZ LU7 ... 2
Ormsby Cl LTN LU1 ... 5
Orpington Cl LTNW/LEA LU4 ... 4
Osborne Rd DUN/WHIP LU6 ...
LTN LU1 ...
Osborn Rd AMP/FLIT/BLC MK45 ...
Otterton Cl HARP AL5 ... 7
Oulton Ri HARP AL5 ... 7
Ouseley Cl LTNW/LEA LU4 ... 4
Overfield Rd LTNE LU2 ... 4
Overstone Rd HARP AL5 ... 7
LTNW/LEA LU4 ... 4
Oving Cl LTNE LU2 ... 4
Oxendon Ct LBUZ LU7 ...
Oxen Rd LTNE LU2 ...
Oxford Rd HTCHE/RSTV SG4 ... 4
LTN LU1 ...
Ox La HARP AL5 ... 7

P

Packhorse Pl DUN/WHIP LU6 * ... 6
Paddock Cl LTNW/LEA LU4 ...
The Paddocks LBUZ LU7 ...
Paddock Vw LTNE LU2 * ...
Paddock Wd HARP AL5 ...
Paignton Cl LTNW/LEA LU4 ...
Paisley Cl LTNW/LEA LU4 ...
Palma Cl DUN/WHIP LU6 ...
Palmer Crs LBUZ LU7 ...
The Parade DUN/WHIP LU6 * ...
LTNN/LIM LU3 ...
Park Av DUN/HR/TOD LU5 ...
DUN/WHIP LU6 ...
LTNN/LIM LU3 ...
Park Av North HARP AL5 ...
Park Av South HARP AL5 ...
Park Cl STALW/RED AL3 ...
Parkfield STALW/RED AL3 ...
Park Hl DUN/HR/TOD LU5 ...
HARP AL5 ...
Parkland Dr LTN LU1 ...
Park La DUN/WHIP LU6 ...
Park Leys DUN/HR/TOD LU5 ...
Park Meadow Cl
AMP/FLIT/BLC MK45 ...
Park Mt HARP AL5 ...
Park Ri HARP AL5 ...
Park Rise Cl HARP AL5 ...
Park Rd AMP/FLIT/BLC MK45 ...
DUN/HR/TOD LU5 ...
DUN/HR/TOD LU5 ...
Park Rd North
DUN/HR/TOD LU5 ...
Parkside Cl
DUN/HR/TOD LU5 ...
Parkside Dr
DUN/HR/TOD LU5 ...
Park St DUN/WHIP LU6 ...
LTN LU1 ...
Park St West LTN LU1 ...
Park Ter LTN LU1 ...
The Park STALW/RED AL3 ...
Park Viad LTN LU1 ...
Park View Cl LTNN/LIM LU3 ...
Park View Dr STALW/RED AL3 ...
Parkview La LBUZ LU7 ...
Parkway Rd LTN LU1 ...
Parrot Cl DUN/HR/TOD LU5 ...
Partridge Cl LTNW/LEA LU4 ...
Parva Cl HARP AL5 ...
Parys Rd LTNN/LIM LU3 ...
Pascomb Rd DUN/WHIP LU6 ...
Pasture La HTCHE/RSTV SG4 ...
The Pastures DUN/WHIP LU6 ...
Pastures Wy LTNW/LEA LU4 ...
Patterdale Cl DUN/WHIP LU6 ...
Peach Ct LTN LU1 ...
Peartree Cl DUN/HR/TOD LU5 ...
Pear Tree La LBUZ LU7 ...
Peartree Rd LTNE LU2 ...
Pebblemoor DUN/WHIP LU6 ...
Peck Ct AMP/FLIT/BLC MK45 ...
Peddars La LBUZ LU7 ...

Schools address data provided by Education Direct.

Petrol station information supplied by Johnsons.

Garden centre information provided by:

Garden Centre Association   Britains best garden centres

Wyevale Garden Centres

The statement on the front cover of this atlas is sourced, selected and quoted
from a reader comment and feedback form received in 2004

SPEED READING

Speed camera locations

Speed camera locations provided in association with RoadPilot Ltd

RoadPilot is the developer of one of the largest and most accurate databases of speed camera locations in the UK and Europe. It has provided the speed camera information in this atlas. RoadPilot is the UK's pioneer and market leader in GPS (Global Positioning System) road safety technologies.

microGo (pictured right) is RoadPilot's latest in-car speed camera location system. It improves road safety by alerting you to the location of accident black spots, fixed and mobile camera sites. RoadPilot's microGo does not jam police lasers and is therefore completely legal.

RoadPilot's database of fixed camera locations has been compiled with the full co-operation of regional police forces and the Safety Camera Partnerships.

For more information on RoadPilot's GPS road safety products, please visit **www.roadpilot.com** or telephone 0870 240 1701

RoadPilot

ALARM MO

GPS Antenna
microGo is directional, it only alerts you to cameras on your side of the road

Visual Countdown
To camera location

Your Speed
The speed you are travelling when approaching camera

Camera Types Located
Gatso, Specs, Truvelo, TSS/DSS, Traffipax, mobile camera sites, accident black spots, congestion charges, tolls

Voice Warnings
Only if you are exceeding the speed limit at the camera

Plug and Go
Easy to move from vehicle to vehicle

64 Colour Options
To match vehicle's illumination

Speed Limit at Came
Screen turns red as additional visual ale

Single Button Operation
For easy access to speed display, camera warning, rescue me location, trip computer, congestion charge, max speed alarm, date and time

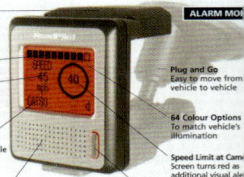